A Coach's Faith

A True Story of How a Football Coach
Made Something Out of Nothing
Through His Faith in Jesus

By Tim Freeman
Praise for Coach Freeman

"Words cannot express my gratitude for Coach Tim Freeman and what his program did for me. For a guy like me, it was a second chance--maybe even a last chance." --James Draine
Mt. Olive Prep Academy 2003-2004,
Fayetteville State University

"Without Coach Freeman, I would never have received a full scholarship to attend Howard College, which was ranked as the #1 junior college in the country when I signed to play there the following year. Coach made me believe that nothing is impossible!"--Shasta Scott
North Atlanta Prep Academy 2005-06,
Howard College Junior College, Point University

"Coach Freeman taught me how to learn from my mistakes and try to make things right. His program gave me hope."
--Teron Williams
Chattahoochee Tech 211-2013,
Clark Atlanta University

"After two years with Coach Freeman, I was able to walk away with a scholarship to Western Kentucky, an associate degree in business management, and the knowledge of what to expect at the next stage in my life."--Cedric Stadom

Chattahoochee Technical College 2011-2013,

Western Kentucky University

"Coach Freeman gave me a second chance to re-establish my academic GPA and another opportunity to play football at the next level."--Morgan Wright

Chattahoochee Technical College 2011-2013,

Tusculum College

Copyright 2014 by Tim Freeman

A Coach's Faith, by Tim Freeman

ISBN 978-1-63068-811-0 (Soft Cover)

All rights reserved solely by the author. The author guarantees that all contents are original and do not infringe upon the legal rights of any other person or work. No part of this book may be reproduced in any form without the permission of the author.

Unless otherwise indicated, Bible quotations are taken from the New Revised Standard Version of the Bible. Copyright © 1999 by Oxford University Press, Inc.

www.CoachFreeman.com

Cover design by Essence Williams

It was highly unlikely that I--someone with a learning disability who struggled to get through school himself--would be the one God chose to help struggling kids get into college and bring many of them to Christ. It was also highly unlikely that being dyslexic, I would write a book about it. God chose unlikely people throughout the Bible to do His work, and He continues to do so today.

"But you be watchful in all things, endure afflictions, do the work of an evangelist, fulfill your ministry."--2 Timothy 4:5

A Coach's Faith

Chapter 1

Week one

On July 13, 2011, we held our first meeting team meeting. It was the start of our second season of the Chattahoochee Technical College Club Football Team, a small school in Marietta, Georgia, a suburb of Atlanta. This was the first day of our conditioning program for the 2011 season, and the team met in our newly renovated weight room, which before the renovation was a shell of a garage in a metal utility building. This would be my first opportunity to address the team as a whole.

The first thing I explained to them was that our program was built on 2 Corinthians 5:7, which says, "For we walk by faith, not by sight." I said this because God had put on my heart to teach young men what true faith is, as it is stated in Hebrews 11:1: "Faith is the substance of things hoped for but evidence of things not yet seen." Then I broke down the verses to how they pertained to our football program and our goal, which was to win the National Club Football Association championship. But this it was July, and the national championship would not be decided until December. "The championship is the thing we're hoping for," I told them "but because it's five months away, it's also the evidence of the thing not yet seen. If we walk in faith for five months and believe in faith that the championship will be ours in the end, then our faith will see us through all the obstacles that might come our way during the season." I ended our morning talk with a prayer of faith.

Then we got our conditioning program started. We began with 74 players in the program. By club football standards, we were loaded with talent. We had only three players returning from the 2010 team, which had a 4-4 record, finishing 7th nationally. We had signed eleven players during spring tryouts and fifty freshmen. We had ten players who

A Coach's Faith

had academic situations they had to work out who would be joining the team two weeks later.

The conditioning program was intense. Because our weight room was small, we had the offense go in for an hour while the defense stayed on the field doing drills. Then after an hour we switched them out.

The first day was a success. Everyone finished the workout. As a coaching staff, we were very pleased with what we saw. We wrapped up the conditioning period the same way we started: with a prayer of thanks to God.

I thought back to 1994 and how events back then began to put me on the path to where I stood today. Back then, every Sunday in church our pastor would say that if you walk by faith and not by sight, something good is going to happen to you. But that Sunday it really hit me. I decided that I was going to step out on faith and quit my other job so I could take a firefighter class. I prayed, and I said to God, "I trust you to provide my every need."

Tim Freeman

On the third Tuesday in February 1994, I started firefighter rookie school. God is so great. On my second day of class I was telling one of my classmates that I had quit my job to do the classes. He said he was the manager of the Loss Prevention Department at JC Penney's in the nearby mall and was looking for someone to help with security. I took the job. The firefighter classes were a lot harder than I thought they would be, and at one point I thought about giving up. Then I thought about our Sunday school slogan: *If I put my mind to it, I can do it and I shall do it.* Every time classes or the hands-on training got hard, I would repeat that slogan over and over again to myself.

Three months into our class we were allowed to start doing ride-alongs with the full-timers on the engines. What I would do was sleep at the station and ride along if there was a call so I could get as much training as possible. I completed the firefighter training in August 1994 and received my firefighter certification.

After that came the opportunity every rookie firefighter lived for: training to drive the fire engine, which would last another three months. There were thirteen people in our class. Because I knew I had a learning disability, I stayed at the station as much as possible to study with the full-timers and watch what they were doing. I figured this would help me absorb what I needed to learn. The first time, I was with my cousin Todd and his partner. Todd was driving that day. I had my learner's permit, so I asked him if I could drive the engine to get fuel at Station 1, which was about five miles away. There was a long pause. Finally, he said okay and started to climb into the back seat. "If we wreck," he joked, "I don't want to see it coming."

His partner got in the front seat, turned to me, and said, "The first time you scare me, your driving days are over." I was excited, but I was also nervous, and on the way I got too close to the edge of the road and ran over some of the safety bumps. The guys started screaming like I was driving off a cliff. Then they began to laugh hysterically. When we arrived at Station 1, as I was backing the engine in, I brushed the curb. "We're gonna need to get curb-finders for the engine when you drive," said Todd, laughing. When we finally got back to Station 4, Todd and his partner jumped out and started kissing the ground. I took their ribbing in stride. I was just happy to have had the chance to drive.

When it came time for the final test, there were three parts: written, practical, and driving. Out of the thirteen in my class, I was the only one to pass all three parts.

Chapter 2

In September of 1995, I enrolled in school to get my Emergency Medical Technician (EMT) certification. During EMT School, I was watching TV one day and saw an interview with KRS-1 from the rap group Boogie Down Productions. The interviewer asked KRS-1, "How have you stayed so successful over the years?" He answered, "The way people stay successful is that when they make it to the top, they continue to repeat the steps that got them there." Then he gave an example: "If you got up at 5 a.m. to start the day and worked 10-12 hours to get where you are, you don't stop that. You repeat the process."

With this in mind, I repeated the process that had gotten me through my firefighter training and my EMT training--staying at the station as much as possible to be around people who could help me study for my state boards, which were coming up in December. I had a job waiting for me if I passed the test.

One night I was at the station studying for the big test. I had books and notes spread all over the table when one of the veteran firefighters walked in.

"What are you doing?" he asked.

"Studying for my EMT board exam," I said. He shook his head.

"You're not going to pass by going over everything like that." he said. "Look, there are only a hundred questions on the test. Here's what you have to do: Go through each chapter of your book, and pick out the most important information on each subject." I went back over all the material and did what he told me to do. There were two parts to the test: written and practical. I passed written part but made one mistake on the practical that caused me to fail. I explained to the test administrator that I had a job offer that depended on my passing this test. He made a call to my instructor from class, who told him I had not had any problems with the practice check-off we had in class. So he let me redo that section. This time I passed, and I received my EMT certification.

The following Monday I went to fill out the paperwork for my job. They asked for a seven-year driving history, and when they turned it in to the insurance company, they were told I had too many points on my driving record to be added to the company's insurance policy. Fortunately, one of my tickets was going to be removed from my record in a month, and I was able to start at the ambulance service in February 1996. Things were going well. God was putting me in favor with the right people. I was working full time with the ambulance service and doing 12-hour volunteer shifts at the fire department that initially paid $50 per shift and later jumped to $75. I got an apartment and bought a used Toyota pickup truck. My five-year-old daughter would frequently tease me about that truck. She'd say, "Daddy, you're a big man. When are you going to get a big-man truck?" I would

Tim Freeman

always answer, "When Daddy starts making some big-man money."

Then the devil started playing tricks on me. Instead of being happy with the blessings I had, I wanted more. And there was nothing I wanted more than to be a full-time firefighter. I must have put in an application with every fire department in the state of Georgia. Most of them had a standardized test you had to pass, and I failed several of them. The devil put it in my mind that I would never get a job with the fire department. He was telling me I should just give up. I started to think that people didn't like me. Because of self-imposed stress and a bad diet, I started to have acid reflux along with anxiety attacks that eventually developed into high blood pressure. I got it in my head that I was going to die of a heart attack any minute. It did not help that I had tendonitis in my left shoulder from an old high school football injury. So every time I felt a reflux episode or shoulder pain, I went to the hospital thinking I was dying.

A Coach's Faith

But I was still praying regularly, and every day I would read my Bible and fight my way through the day. In July, I was able to get a job interview with the City of Woodstock for a full-time firefighter position. After I had gone through the interview, the background check, and the physical agility parts of the hiring process, I got a phone call from the assistant chief there. He said it had come down to me and another guy, and he said they offered him the position. He then said I was next in line, and if they had an opening in the next twelve months, they would hire me. I was at peace with that because I felt in my spirit that it was okay.

Still, I continued to apply at different fire departments. In March of the following year, I tested for a full-time position with the City of Alpharetta, where I had been a volunteer for more than two years, as well as in Douglas County. I failed both tests. When I got the results, I had a nervous breakdown. I quit my job with the ambulance service and the volunteer fire department. I was fed up. I

Tim Freeman

figured I'd never be able to pass the test, and I moved back home with my mother. I just could not take failing again.

A couple of months later, I started working full-time for a local tool rental company, delivering equipment to construction sites. I was slowly getting over the letdown of not working for the fire department, but deep down inside I still wanted to be a firefighter. It was the first time in my life that I had worked hard for something--certification as a firefighter--that I felt would really make a difference in my life.

In mid-July, I had to make a delivery in Woodstock, and on my way back to the office I needed to use the bathroom. I spotted a fire station, went in, and asked if I could use their bathroom. As I was washing my hands, I thought I heard someone say, "That's him!" When I came out of the restroom, one of the firefighters asked me my name. When I told him, he said, "We've been looking for you."

I wasn't sure what he was talking about, but he asked if I could wait there while he made a phone call. A few minutes later, the assistant fire chief walked in.

"Man, you're a hard person to find," he said. Then he told me that one of his firefighters was leaving to go to another department and that they had been looking for me take his place. Here's where God is in this. If I had not taken that delivery, I would not have gotten the job as a firefighter because there was only one week left in the 12-month period when they would have had to hire the next person on the list. In God's plan and his time, he put me in the right place at the right moment to receive my blessing. On August 9, 1997, I worked my first full-time shift as a paid firefighter.

That first year, I received the firefighter of the year award. At the time, the City of Woodstock only had one fire station. I had come from a city that had four. As a result, I knew more about how to use equipment such as the new ladder we had just purchased. Woodstock was getting more and more apartment complexes, and I knew a lot about fighting fires in larger structures such as high-rises. Because I had this knowledge, they often came to me with questions. I also conducted fire-safety education at elementary schools and nursing homes.

On my first shift, my partner for the day was a 12-year veteran named Craig.

"Just remember one thing, rookie," he said sternly in his Queens, New York, accent. "That broom in the corner has more seniority than you do." After that, I got settled in and bonded with the rest of the guys.

Chapter 3

Everything was going great. I was not having anxiety attacks as much. God was showing me favor. But there was something missing. So I started praying that God would send me a wife. One day in June of 1998, I was doing driver training with a rookie firefighter in the department in an old squad truck that had no air conditioning. For some reason, we decided to go into Wal-Mart to get out of the heat. Before I got out of the truck, God spoke to me. "Your wife is in Wal-Mart," God said. *Okay*, I thought, not really sure I was hearing from God. Sure enough, behind the jewelry counter stood a beautiful young lady named Melanie, who I did marry a little more than a year later on August 30, 1999. My daughter was nine, and Melanie had an eight-year-old son and a seven-year-old daughter. On July 24, 1999 God blessed us with another beautiful daughter. Also in July of 1999 we purchased our own house and a minivan.

I would work a 24-hour shift at the fire department, and then be off for 48 hours. On my days off, I worked part time delivering fire extinguishers for a fire protection company. In my spare time, I would help my cousins who were in high school try to get recruited by colleges to play football. While on one college visit, I made friends with a coach who helped me get a part-time job with a recruiting service out of Birmingham, Alabama, called the National Scouting Report. In April of 2000 I quit my job with the fire protection company and went to work part time at the Roswell Fire Department. I was living the dream. I got to drive a fire engine three days a week and watch sports on the other days--plus I got paid for it.

Four months later, my life was forever changed. While fighting a house fire, I fell down six steps in full firefighter gear, fracturing two bones in the lower lumbar region of my back. During three months of physical therapy I

A Coach's Faith

was put on workers compensation, which was about $200 less per week than I had been making, Because I could no longer work for the Roswell Fire Department and the scouting service, it didn't take long for the bills to start piling up and the stress to start building. After six months of physical therapy, I took an agility test to see if I was ready to return to work at the fire department. The good news was that I was able to pass the test and return to work. The bad news was that on my first shift back, I reinjured my back helping to lift a patient. After seeing the doctor, I was put on light duties, which at a fire department meant that I was basically doing the work of a secretary.

I wasn't happy about it, but what made things worse was that sitting all day made my back hurt. I was about to learn one of my biggest life lessons. My chief and assistant chief called me in for a meeting.

"I only have one concern," the assistant chief said. "And it's that when the alarm goes off there are enough firefighters on that truck." I understood his position. I would have felt the same way. His statement showed me something that I teach every young man I come in contact with: Anyone can be replaced, so you should always be working to better yourself. I was put back on workers compensation while our lawyer and the fire department's lawyer worked out a settlement.

I had been out of a job before. But this was different. Now I had a family.

While all of this was going on, I would still work with a few kids from my church, trying to help them get athletic scholarships to college. I was praying to God to show what me next move would be. Some of these kids had come up short on their SAT or ACT scores, and their Core GPAs were too low for them to be eligible to participate as a freshman in NCAA Divisions 1 and II.

I started researching alternative opportunities that could help them if they were not eligible to participate as freshmen. I found out about a private school in the northeast that had high school post-graduate programs. If a student-athlete did not graduate from high school, he could do a post-graduate year, which was basically a fifth year of high school. As an NCAA non-qualifier, a student-athlete could retake core classes he or she may have failed or received a low grade in to help raise their core GPA to meet NCAA freshmen eligibility standards. They also could retake the SAT or ACT test to try to raise their score. The best part was that the post-graduate year did not count against a student athlete's NCAA eligibility, which it would if they attended a junior college.

The problem for the student I was helping was that he could not afford the $25,000 tuition to attend. And because it was a high school, there wasn't any financial aid available other than a $2,500 scholarship. His family would have to come up with the rest. God gave me the vision of starting a similar post-graduate program in Georgia that would be affordable for student-athletes and their families. After lots of prayer, meditation, and research, I wrote out a proposal of what it would cost to do a post-graduate program for football players. Habakkuk 2:2 says, "Write the vision and make it plain on tablets, that he may run who reads it."

Unfortunately, the football program was too expensive. So God redirected my vision to fit his plan. He gave me the vision of doing a basketball program, which would be about one-fourth the cost of the football program. Through this program not only would I be developing great student-athletes, I would also be developing young men who would have a strong spiritual foundation and character. God showed me how all the things I had been through had prepared me for this journey. I was to build this program on faith and teach the kids what true faith is. Remember the verse I mentioned earlier? Hebrews 11:1: "Now faith is the substance of things hoped for, the evidence of things not seen."

All the young men I had dealt with in the past would say, "I'm a grown man," whenever I would try to teach or correct them. The Lord put on my heart to teach them what a true man is, using 1 Corinthian 13:11: "When I was a child I spoke as child, I thought as a child; when I became a man, I put away childish things." I took my vision to the pastor of the church I was attending, and he approved the idea. He brought on board Dr. Mamie Ware, who was a member of the church and second in charge in the education department at Life University. I told them that my vision was to start a post-graduate basketball program with twelve local players who could live at home. We would provide them with SAT and ACT prep classes and a biblically based life-skills class, which we would require all of our kids to take. If one of them needed additional academic classes, he could take them at his local high school.

We had SAT and ACT classes on Wednesday night in the church basement and Saturday morning in the classroom at the rec center before practice. We practiced on Saturday and Sunday for three hours. We would only play 12 games, and only with opponents within a three-hour driving distance from the church. The games were to get the students exposure and game film to show college recruiters. The plan was simple. Then I told the plan to Dr. Ware.

"Let me get this right," she said. "You're going to take a group kids that did not do what they were supposed to do in school and get them ready for college in one year?"

"Correct," I said, eager to hear what she would say next.

"Wrong!" she said sternly. "That's not going to work."

Rather than be discouraged, I told myself that her words only confirmed that this was what God wanted. I knew this because logically she was right. But God's way thinking doesn't rely on logic. God's work relies on the spirit.

Even though Mrs. Ware doubted us, she gave us the chance to try. We did not charge the kids a team fee. We operated on faith for the funding. Initially, I was able to recruit eight local players. On the second Saturday of September 2001, our new program, which we named Mount Olive Prep Academy, held its first SAT prep class and

A Coach's Faith

basketball practice at the Cherokee County Recreation Center in Woodstock, Georgia.

Chapter 4

God had really blessed us with some great athletes. Fortunately for them, I learn very quickly, because their basketball skills were much better than my basketball-coaching skills. I soon realized that I needed to find a real head coach. The next day while we were practicing, I noticed that T.J. Vines, a local high school basketball star who had just graduated from Georgia Tech, was playing in the gym where we were practicing. He came over and started talking with me about the team, and gave me a few pointers on the play we were running. After he left, one of our players asked me, "Can he coach us?" Apparently, my players had also recognized my shortcomings as a coach.

I knew for sure I needed help, so I prayed that God would send someone who would share my vision. The next Sunday at practice I noticed a tall skinny guy training a group of girls. When he gave the girls a break, I went over and spoke with him about what we were doing with the program. It turned out his name was Kenny Jones, a former a NBA player in the mid-1990s. I asked him if he would be interested in coaching my team. He immediately answered "yes," which was a godsend because we only had two weeks before our first game.

The week before our first game, the pastor at my church managed to get an article written about us in the Cherokee County section of the *Atlanta Journal-Constitution* newspaper. The headline read "Mt. Olive Prep Gives One More Chance." Not only did this give our program wider exposure, it would also bring a lot more people out to watch us play. The week of our first game, however, one of our players broke his ankle playing in a pick-up game. That left us with only seven players available for the big game. On November 3, 2001 we played our first game versus South Georgia Tech, which also happened to be playing the first game in their program's history. They beat us 89-53. We

A Coach's Faith

knew the first thing we had to do was get more players. Chuck Davis, who ran the Marietta Heat AAU basketball program where five of our players also played, called me and said. "I'd like to help you, Coach. I know some more players who'd like to play for you."

The next week Chuck set us up with four new players. He also arranged for us to be able to practice at the Boys & Girls Club in Marietta, which made it a lot easier for the players to get back and forth to practices, since most of them lived near there. The church pastor's dad was a pastor of a church in Birmingham, and his church donated a 12-passenger van to our church, which our church agreed to let us use for road trips. All we would have to do was provide gas money.

It seemed that all the pieces were falling into place. But the first time we took the team on the road, we realized that a 12-passenger van was too small for 12 large young men—four of whom were over 6'5"—and two coaches. So what we did was to let one of the players drive my wife's van and take four players, while I took the rest in the church van. Money got so tight that one trip I had to go around my neighborhood to collect pennies for gas. After that, I would get people I knew to sponsor trips. God always gave us favor with the right people.

One week, I could not find a sponsor for a three-hour trip we had scheduled to Maryville, Tennessee, to play the Maryville College JV team, and it looked like we were going to have to cancel the game. I prayed to God and asked him what I should do. God said, "Go." So I left home with $20 in my pocket and went to meet the team. On my way, I got a call from my wife. "Aunt Maggie called," she said, "and told me that God told her to give you $50." It was perfect timing because I was one exit from her house. I knew it had to be God.

In the second week, we got a transfer student named Clark Williams, a shooting guard who had been one of the state's top high school recruits. He had been attending a prep school in Massachusetts but needed SAT prep and wanted to

A Coach's Faith

be closer to home. Every time we had a game, college coaches would be there to see him. He was a lights-out three-point shooter who made an immediate impact on our team. His presence inspired the other players and lifted their game as well. At the end of the year we had an open gym for college coaches come to watch our guy's play. To my surprise there were recruiters from such big-name schools as the University of South Carolina, East Carolina, University of Virginia, and Tennessee Tech there. We went on to have successful first year, finishing 8-4. Eight of our players moved on to junior colleges, three moved up to four-year colleges, and one joined the U.S. Army.

While it seemed that everything was going okay with the program, the season of Job was beginning at home. I had gotten a small settlement from the fire department, but the money was running out. I had started an auto-detailing business that was doing really well before the 9/11 bombing of the World Trade Center. After 9/11, business dried up. In the wake of the terror attack, people were being careful with their money, and detailing is a luxury rather than a necessity. I eventually had to close shop and tried doing a mobile detailing business for a while. My best friend, Elbert Shelley, who had a limo business, hired me to clean his cars and set me up with one of his clients to keep their cars clean. But it wasn't enough. Because of my back injury, I had to use helpers, which I could no longer afford, so I had to close my detail business.

I was struggling to provide for my family, but I knew God had a plan for me. I was going to do his will, no matter what. I took a job selling alarm systems door-to-door, and I also started delivering newspapers to make some extra money. Still, my one true passion was building the post-grad basketball program, so in every free moment I studied the NCAA rule book on eligibility and recruiting. It was also a season of division at the church. The battle was that the church was over 100 years old in a small town where most of the members had been in that church of all their lives and they did not like the changes the new pastor wanted to make, which included attracting new members. It got so bad that the old-timers would sit on the left side of the church, and the newcomers would sit on the right.

In the spring of 2002 the pastor left Mt. Olive Baptist Church to start his own church. My family and I started attending a different church, and I moved the whole program to Marietta, where we were already practicing. We were able to use a couple of classrooms at a nearby tech school. Word about the program was spreading, and in the summer of 2002 I got phone call from the head basketball coach at Furman University. He was coming to Atlanta on a recruiting trip and wanted to meet with me. We met at the Boys & Girls Club.

He asked me to explain how our program worked. I told him I did SAT and ACT prep and life skills through our Bible life-studies class. That was it. He said it was a perfect fit for what he was looking for. He had a 6'9" kid from Africa who was currently in a private school in Louisiana, and he wanted to send him to play for us. If we could help this kid get at least an 820 on his SATs to qualify for NCAA freshmen eligibility, the Furman coach would sign him for the next season. I agreed to take him because I knew that having a player of his quality would greatly enhance the program. I was starting to get phone calls from other college coaches, AAU coaches, and parents wanting to send kids to our program. I had no idea where these people were getting my phone number.

Now we had two new challenges: If we took kids from outside the area, how would we feed and house them?

Chapter 5

I drove all around the area trying to find a place close to the college where we had class and the Boys & Girls club. I found some studio-style apartments that we could put two people in that were very affordable. That solved one problem. But how would they eat? The apartments were right across the street from the college, so I went to head of the food services at the college and asked him if could give us a deal on meal tickets for our players. He did, which solved problem number two.

Mossua, the kid from Africa who the Furman coach had told me about, came to live with me and my family in August of 2002 because his time was up with his host family in Louisiana. I knew there was going to be one major hurdle I had to get over to be able to have Mossua live with us. That hurdle was my wife. When I asked Melanie if it would be okay for Mossua to live with us for three days until I could

Tim Freeman

find a place for him to live, she said her main concerns were that we didn't know him at all and how could we afford to feed him and our three kids? I assured her it would only be three days.

She leaned her head to the side. "Three days? Yeah, right."

I gave her my begging puppy dog look and said, "Pleeeze?"

"Okay," she said. "Three days!"

I picked Moussa up from the bus station and brought him to the house with me. He met my family, and he and my 3-year-old daughter immediately fell in love with each other. She would call him "Mossua the Mossua" (pronounced Moose-a the Moose-a), and he would call her "Choo-Choo the Choo-Choo." He fit in very well with our family. I took Mossua to the immigration department to do the paperwork for his resident status and after several interviews I was able to get him a visa to stay in the country.

A Coach's Faith

One day our electricity was turned off, and I was embarrassed to tell Mossua it was because of we hadn't been able to pay our electric bill. Instead, I told him that the lights were off in the whole neighborhood and that we would have to stay with my mother-in-law until the power company restored our power. I was blessed to get the money from my mom the next day, and we were able to return home. Even though Mossua's three-day visit turned into three weeks, Melanie told me the day Mossua was leaving that she thought he was a very nice, neat, and well-mannered young man. She actually said it had been a blessing to have him stay with us.

The big turning point in our program came when Mossua got his SAT score back. It was exactly 820. At the time, the coaching staff at Furman and I thought the score was not high enough for him to be eligible to play. So Furman allowed him to enroll in school as a non-qualifier, which meant he would be able to practice with the team but not be able to play in games. About four months later, I got a letter from the NCAA informing me about their new rules for freshmen eligibility. I saw that under the new rules, as long as he had a 2.5 core GPA and an SAT score of at least 820, Mossua was eligible to play as a freshman. I immediately called Furman's head coach and gave him the good news. The fall semester had just begun and they were still a month from their first game. Mossua made the All-Conference Freshman team and did well in school that year.

That same year, we had three players sign scholarships with Division 1 colleges. This really helped the program grow. Once word got out that we could help players become eligible, everyone wanted to send kids to us. In April 2003, the day after signing day, I got fifty-three phone calls about players. There was one player we really wanted. His name was Rashaun Bryant. He was 6'8" and 260 lbs. He had signed a scholarship to play with the University of Colorado. Once again we had landed one of the top players in the state.

In 2003 we also landed a very good point guard named James Parker from North Cobb Christian School. James was only 5'10," but he could virtually jump out of the

A Coach's Faith

gym. I was introduced to James by friend of mine named Walter Jordan, who was an assistant at the boy's school. Walter, a former NBA player who was well connected with some of the parents of the kids he coached, took a strong interest in the program. He introduced me to his friend Gary, who had an incredible vision for the AAU program Gary ran. Gary also took a strong interest in our program and showed me the blueprints of his vision of a sports complex he was going to build that had a gym, as well as baseball, soccer, and football fields. It also had classrooms and a chapel. He told me he wanted to include my program as a part of his vision. This was the answer to my prayers. I told Gary about the Bible life studies class we were doing, and he recommended his secretary to teach the class for us. That year 12 out of 14 players in her class gave their life to Christ.

In the summer of 2003, because of our family financial situation, our house got foreclosed on, and we had to move out of our house and move in with my mother and sister. I will never forget that day. The doorbell rang, I looked out the peephole, and saw a sheriff's deputy standing on the front porch. When I opened the door, he introduced himself and handed me an envelope. "I'm sorry to tell you this," he said, "but your house was sold in a public foreclosure auction on the Cherokee County Courthouse steps. You have 10 days to move out." The day before were moved out, Melanie and I sat down and talked about the move. As difficult as this was, we both felt we were at peace with the situation.

But on the day of the move, Melanie said she couldn't help feeling angry and bitter. "This wasn't supposed to be our life," she said. As we packed our things, she would be in one room and I would be in another, but both of us were shedding tears. We had lost everything. Our van was repossessed, and I had a 1977 Olds Cutlass--my dream car--that my uncle had given to me. I had planned to restore it when we got back on our feet, but it wasn't running, and I had to get it out of the driveway before we had to move, so I gave it to the Tommy Nobis Foundation, and organization founded by former Atlanta Falcons linebacker to provide job training, employment, and vocational support for youth and adults with disabilities and other barriers to employment. But even though I knew the car was going to good cause, when I watched tow truck pull off, I couldn't help but think: *I'm such a loser I couldn't even keep what was given to me.*

Chapter 6

We moved to Duluth with my mom, which meant I would now have to drive thirty miles each way to keep the program going. Despite all the chaos in my personal life, we had a good basketball season as a team, although Rashaun did not have the individual numbers we had hoped for. Plus, even though he had earned a qualifying SAT, the NCAA flagged his scores because he had made too big a jump from his high school SAT scores. I filed an appeal with NCAA showing that he had taken an intense SAT prep class to prepare for the test, but they denied the appeal. He was allowed to take the test again, but this time he was unable to make the necessary score to qualify to play as a freshman. Colorado pulled their scholarship offer, and he ended up going to Tennessee Tech. We did, however, have eleven other guys sign scholarships that spring.

While all this was going on, I was also coaching an AAU basketball team for my friend Gary's program. Things went well with the team. I had told Gary about my being foreclosed on, and out of the blue he called and said, "I have friend with a condo in Marietta that's sitting empty. If you'd like to move your family in there, you can work for me to pay your rent." At that moment, I thanked God profusely. I love my mother and sister, you understand, but it's just hard to live with relatives when they're used to having their own space.

We moved into the condo, and everything was going okay. Then Gary had to go into the hospital to have surgery to repair a leaking heart valve. He had what is commonly known as Abraham Lincoln's disease. During surgery, Gary had a major stroke and died two days later. He had become a very good friend. Losing him was like losing a member of the family. After talking it over with Walter, he advised me to continue my program to honor Gary's spirit. My family and I were able to stay in the condo for three months before we had to leave and move in with my mother-in-law in Woodstock.

A Coach's Faith

My wife and I decided to leave our kids in school in Marietta, so they would not have to start a new school. For the entire second semester, I drove my kids to school in Marietta and picked them up in the afternoon. We had a one child in preschool, one in elementary, and one in middle school.

As I started preparing for year four with our program, I realized that with the recognition we were getting that it was time to add accredited classes—English, math, social studies, science, and Spanish—to the program. It was time to go from being an SAT and ACT preparatory program to a full-fledged school. I had been studying the NCAA rules on freshmen and what a student athlete could do in a post-graduate year to raise his GPA. The main thing I had to do was get our new school accredited.

I did some research and found the Georgia Accrediting Commission, which accredited most of the state's private schools. They also accredited non-traditional schools, which are basically places where home-schooled students meet once a week to get tutoring or other kinds of help with their classes. I called Dr. Ware and asked if she would be willing to sign off on the accrediting commission application as Director of Academics. She said would, but she was not going to be able to attend the meeting the day the accrediting commission was coming for the site visit. The Boys & Girls Club had agreed to let us use the classroom during the morning hours when they were not using them. I made sure we had all our paperwork in line. In our second year of the program, we had already received our College Board school code and had been approved as an SAT testing site. So I felt we were in a good position. I can't remember ever being as nervous as I was on the day of the site visit. It was raining and dreary. I prayed to God, "I know Dr. Ware can't be here, but I know you are here with me. Please guide me through this meeting. In the end, let your will be done."

When the site evaluator arrived, he turned out to be one of the nicest people I had ever met. He was an older gentleman who had retired from teaching. I explained the program to him and what we were trying to do with it. He

A Coach's Faith

loved the idea. Then we toured the facility, and at the end of the tour he told me he would recommend us for accreditation. As I drove home, I was thanking God for his mercy and grace. Suddenly, it stopped raining and the sun began to shine. Two months later, we got formal approval from the NCAA Clearinghouse. They would accept all the academic courses we were offering for NCAA freshmen eligibility.

My next hurdle was getting the paperwork done for our application for 501(c)3 non-profit status. Lots of companies and individuals had been telling me that once we became a non-profit, they would donate to the program. The cost of having 501(c)3 paperwork done by a lawyer was $2,000-$4,000, and it typically took six months to a year to be approved. For one thing, I did not have that kind of money. One day something told me to look at my junk mail instead of throwing it away. There was flyer from a company that would do 501(c)3 paperwork for $300. I called and set up an appointment to meet with him. I showed him all my documents for the program, and he said all I had to do was put together a board of directors and get a Dun & Bradstreet number. Once I did that, he said, he would be able to do our application, and we would have it back in six to eight weeks. I asked him how he could do it so cheaply and get it back so quickly. He said it was all about doing the application right the first time. When you do it wrong, the IRS up sends it back to you for correction, and that's when lawyer fees build up and the delays occur. Once I got my advisory board names and my Dun & Bradstreet number to him, I received the official 501(c)3 letter determination in four weeks.

One other thing I needed was a physical address for the school. So I rented a one-room office in a nice building just up the street from the Boys & Girls Club. They also had a big classroom in the building that we could use. I bought a new table for the office that had to be assembled. I'm not a handyman by a long shot, so I had my wife come help me put it to together. Later that night she started complaining of stomach pain. I knew something was really wrong when she asked me to take her to the hospital. I dropped her off at the

A Coach's Faith

patient intake desk in the emergency room then went back out to park the car. When I came back in, my wife was not where I left her. When I asked where she was, a nurse grabbed me and said, "Come on," and rushed me up to my wife's room. When I got there, they told me my wife was having a baby. We didn't even know she was pregnant. The first thing my wife said to me was, "What is your mama gonna say?" My response was, "What is *your* mama gonna say?"

About thirty minutes after the baby was born, I got up the nerve to call my mom. She reacted like any proud grandma. She took off work and showed up at the hospital three hours later with some new baby clothes. Right after I talked with my mom, I called my wife's mom. Her first reaction was, "What are we going to name her?" I told her we were going to call here Loren after my dad, whose name was Lorenzo. She then asked, "What's her middle name going to be?" I knew where she was headed, so I quickly responded, "It's gonna be the same as your middle name—Ann." So everybody was happy.

Chapter 7

Because I had to get all the paperwork done on accreditation, I got a late start on recruiting for the 2004-2005 team. I wanted to be able to tell the kids we trying to recruit that we could now offer more than just SAT or ACT prep, which made us much more attractive to potential recruits who needed to raise their core GPAs. Coach Adams, who had been faithful to the program for three years, decided not to return, which meant I had to find a new head coach.

One afternoon I got a call from Garrett Respress, the coach from Tennessee Tech who had recruited Rashaun the year before. Coach Respress had a player he wanted me to take a look at for our program. After I spoke with Coach Respress for a while, he told me he was moving to Atlanta to get married and start his own AAU basketball program. A

Tim Freeman

week later, he came to my office, and I asked him if he would be interested in being head coach of our program.

I showed him our school certification to show we were legit. Then we started working on recruiting some of the players he had his eye on, plus the local players I had already approached. We put together a dream team that featured Curtis Brown Jr., a 6'9" center who had been sought after by every Division 1 school in the country; and Courtni Houston, a dead-eye shooting guard; Dominique Bedford a 240-pound, 6'8" beast of a forward. And then there was Paul Daniels, a true miracle of God. In April of 2003, his sister had gotten into a fight with her boyfriend at the neighborhood recreation center. Paul went there to get his sister, and as they were walking away, her boyfriend hit him in the back of the head with a baseball bat. Paul spent months in the hospital. The doctors said he would be a vegetable for the rest of his life. But God said different. Paul's mother eventually moved a hospital bed into his room and began caring for him at home.

A Coach's Faith

"One morning," she said, "I was in the kitchen cooking breakfast, and I thought I heard something move. I turned around and Paul was standing there. 'What are you cooking?' he asked me. After a few weeks of physical and speech therapy, Paul was back to normal." The accident happened just before the end of the school year, so Paul was not able to graduate, which is why he needed to come to our program. He was a 6'2" small forward and a hard worker.

For the 2004-2005 season, we went from having four players from outside the area to having eight. That meant we needed more housing. We had the same setup as the year before, holding classes in the Southern Polytech Library. The kids lived in the apartment across the street from the college and could get on the school's meal plan. The apartment did not have enough units for all our players, so I found a three-bedroom house to rent that was one street over from the apartment. We could put six players in the house, two to a room. The rent was $800 per month, which would come to $133.33 per month each, plus $50 each for utilities per month, for a total of $183.33 per player. I met with the homeowner, a super nice guy, and I told him all about the program and what we were doing. He agreed to rent the house to us.

The deposit we needed on the house was $1,600, which represented the first and last month's rent. So I called the parents of the players who were going to be living there and told them that their sons had to bring a money order for $267 for his portion of the deposit. I told the homeowner I would write a check for the deposit and asked him to hold it for two weeks until the players arrived. Two weeks passed, and the players started showing up. I saw a couple of kids' parents driving nice SUVs. One parent was driving a brand new Cadillac. I had to pick a couple of the players up from the bus station. Everything seemed to be going okay—until I asked for the deposit money. Only three of the kids had it. The other parents promised they would have it within the next week. I called to let the landlord know what was going on, and he said, "No problem. The guys can go ahead and move in."

A Coach's Faith

We started practice and classes that week. My main goal was to talk to all the people who said they would donate money to the program once we got our 501(c)3 status. I went to everyone I had in my notebook. People made donations, but they were not anywhere near what I thought they would be. Everyone had an excuse. The most common was that the economy was bad and was going to get worse before it got better. This was my first experience with fundraising, and it was a reality check.

We had moved our practices from the Boys & Girls Club to the National Guard Armory because they had a gym with a full-size basketball court. Coach Respress brought in a couple of very good young assistant coaches. One of them was Kevin Young, whose brother was a scout for rivals.com, a major recruiting Web site. Kevin's brother wrote an article on the program, and within two weeks we had college recruiters from all over the country at our practices. At one practice we had recruiters from Purdue, North Carolina, Illinois, Auburn, UNLV, Houston, and Kentucky. Even

Tim Freeman

Tubby Smith, one of the premier basketball coaches in the country, came. After practice, he went around and shook hands with every one of our players. What a humble man. He told me he was very interested in Curtis Brown. In four years we had gone from an unknown grassroots upstart to one of the top post-graduate programs in the county.

Four weeks went by, and I was able to get enough donations, mostly from local businesses, to cover the first month's payroll. But the players who were supposed to come up with their rent deposit did not pay. I went to the homeowner and asked if he could give me another two weeks, which he agreed to do. Two weeks came and went, and we still didn't have the money. The homeowner had the sheriff come and evict the players. I had to ask the players who were living in the apartments to let the evicted players stay with them until I could find another place for them to stay.

Another month went by. Again, the donations did not come in, and I had to make partial payments to my staff. With the financial times we were facing, a couple of coaches had to leave and find more stable work. I fully understood. Our first game came around, and we were forced to play at the local recreation center rather than Southern Poly, where we had been paying to play. We played against Roane State Community College from Tennessee. Roane State had a very good program and had beaten us the last two years. We had lost one assistant coach, but we still managed to beat them. The next week we were scheduled to play in a tournament in Daytona Beach. We didn't have the money to make the trip, so we had to cancel. A couple of players left the team because they couldn't afford to stay in the apartments, and Coach Respress and one of the assistant coaches also left because they weren't able to continue on a partial salary. I had to move our other assistant coach, Kevin Young, to head coach, and a local AAU coach named Don Overall volunteered to step in as his unpaid assistant.

Week three of the season we were to play Georgia Perimeter College, the 11th-ranked junior college team in the county, on a Saturday afternoon. On Friday, Curtis Brown's dad called me, crying. He said that Curtis's aunt in New York had died and that they needed to go up there right away. I told him I was sorry to hear about their loss, and I understood that Curtis had to go be with the family. We lost to Georgia Perimeter by 20 points. Two weeks later I was on the Internet and Googled Curtis's name to see what was going on with his recruitment. A headline came up: CURTIS BROWN COMMITS DURING VISIT. Underneath the headline was a picture of Curtis sitting in the stands at a Kentucky football game. It was the same weekend his aunt was supposed to have died. I phoned his dad and called him every name in the book except "child of God." He told me, "You can't talk to me that way. I'll come get my son." I said, "You don't have to come get him—I'll bring him to you." Once I cooled off, I called him back and said, "You come get him." As mad as I was, I wasn't driving all the way to Savannah, Georgia. I never confronted Curtis because I knew he was only doing what his dad had told him to do.

A Coach's Faith

Before Christmas break, I had a meeting with the staff and players. I told them flat out, "Our bank account is low, and donations are hard to come by. I don't know how things are going to be in January when we return. But if you will stand in faith with me and believe that God will provide for us to complete this year, I will be forever grateful." After the break, two of our four teachers, our assistant coach, and seven of twelve players returned. Three of the players we lost were starters.

Chapter 8

We needed to boost morale, and I knew I had to do something to motivate the kids. So I had my cousin Doby come speak to them about God's favor and how he did everything his own way when he was their age. First, he told them that when he was in high school he was the big man on campus. But when he went to college, he wasn't the big man on campus anymore. He could not handle it and dropped out.

Then he started selling drugs. He went to prison for setting up a drug deal between a friend in California and a friend in North Carolina on a wire-tapped phone. He believed that God put him in prison to speak to him. He told them that once he committed his life to God, God has shown him nothing but favor. Among other things, his sentence was reduced from ten years to three, and his $4 million fine was

Tim Freeman

cut to $100,000. After he got out of prison, he was able to start his own business, get married, and buy a house.

I've seen a lot of people go to prison and say that God changed them, but then within two or three weeks they were back doing the same things. But Doby had been out of prison for six years and had stayed true to his promise to serve God. He created his own prison ministry where he held a Bible study at the county jail every Friday night.

The second half of the year was hard, but with God's favor and our faith we made it. All eight of the players who finished the program received college scholarships. The last game of the season, I coached the best basketball game my life. We played Prince Avenue Prep out of South Carolina. They had fifteen players; we had five. We won by 17 points. There was no finger-pointing or complaining about playing time. Just five guys playing as a team.

During the season, I got call from a friend of mine who was a coach at Kennesaw State. He told me he had a 7'5" kid he wanted me to see and asked if I could come to the gym

A Coach's Faith

right then to meet him. As I was driving there, I was thinking to myself, *This kid better be 7'5."* When I got to the gym, I was sitting in the bleachers and saw the kid come out of the locker room. When he opened the door, I could only see him from the shoulders down. He ducked under the door, and straightened up. He was every bit of 7'5." The guy who brought him to Kennesaw was Mark Vogt. Mark had a big heart and really wanted to help the kids. He wanted success for the kids even more than the kids wanted success for themselves. After we set the kid up with GED classes and had pro trainers work with him for about a month, he went back home to North Carolina for Thanksgiving and never come back.

At the end of the 2004-2005 school year, I decided to change the name of the program from Mt. Olive Prep to North Atlanta Prep. I felt that putting the name Atlanta in the program would raise our profile. At the same time, I moved the program to Mt. Paran North Church of God. LynnBeth McCrener, who was head of their sports ministry, allowed us to use a desk in the church sports ministry office, classrooms where their school used to be, and their gym. This was a perfect fit. Our program finally had a home.

On a Thursday afternoon in 2005, I got a phone call from Mark Vogt, the person who had called me about Tyrone the 7'5" kid. Mark told me he was an owner-operator for Avis Rental Car and that his store was in Marietta, He said that Avis had asked him to take over the Woodstock location and asked me if I'd like to work for him. I immediately said yes. I thanked him and hung up the phone, and I told my wife that I had gotten a real job making real money. We were both excited about the opportunity.

It was only about a 20-minute drive from my house in Canton to Woodstock, but I didn't want to be late so I left my home at noon. As I entered the city limits of Woodstock, I noticed that the traffic was moving slow. I was heading south on Highway 5, and there was a police officer going northbound. When I passed her, I looked in my rearview mirror and saw her turning around with the lights flashing.

A Coach's Faith

She came around a couple of cars and pulled me over. I was thinking to myself, "Just my luck. I can't afford a ticket right now." The officer walked up to my truck and said, "The reason I pulled you over is that I got you on moving radar doing 37 mph in a 25 mph zone." Then she looked at my jacked and saw the City of Woodstock Fire Department patch on my sleeve and said, "I haven't seen you around here before." I told her, that I used to work for the city but I had gotten hurt on the job a couple of years earlier and was ruled physically unable to do the job. She got my license and insurance information and went back to her car. A few minutes later, another police car pulled up. A male cop walk up to the passenger side of my truck as the female came to the driver's side.

"Step out of the vehicle," the female officer said and signaled for me to go around to the other side where her partner was standing.

"What's going on?" I asked her.

"You have a felony warrant out on you from Cobb County."

"For what?" I said. I couldn't think of anything I had done wrong, certainly not a felony.

"I'll explain later," she said. Then the male officer laid me across the trunk of her police, frisked me, and handcuffed me. Just then I saw the assistant fire chief pull up. When he walked over to where we were, the female officer asked him if I had worked for the fire department. He told her I had. I was relieved, but I was also embarrassed to have my former chief see me like that. As she was putting me in the back of her police car, she said, "The warrant is for deposit fraud."

"What does that mean?" I asked her.

"You must have written someone a bad check."

As she transported me back to the Cherokee County jail, I tried to figure out who I could have possibly given a bad check to. When I got to the jail, they showed me the warrant. It was for a check I had written at the beginning of the 2004-

A Coach's Faith

2005 school year for the guys to live in the rental house. I asked the jail deputy what would happen next, and she said I would have to wait for the Cobb County Sheriff's Department to send someone to take me to the Cobb County Jail.

I had arrived at the Cherokee County Jail at 1:30 p.m., and at 4 p.m. they handed me a brown bag dinner.

"Make sure you eat this because this is all you will eat until 5 a.m.," said a deputy. At about 10:30 p.m., a Cobb County officer arrived to pick me up. Twenty minutes later, we pulled into the gate of the Cobb County Jail. I could not help but think, *Lord, why? Why am I going through this? All I have done was try to help these kids. I got all those kids scholarships, and they're all in college, and here I am sitting in jail. Somehow that doesn't seem fair.* I sat in the Cobb County Jail from 11 p.m. till 11 a.m., when my sister came to bail me out. It was the longest 12 hours of my life. Cobb County had run a DUI roadblock around midnight, and at one point I counted 47 people in our tiny holding cell.

A few months later, I had to go to court for arraignment and was assigned a court-appointed lawyer.

"The DA is offering a $1,000 fine and 90 days in jail," he said. "How do want to plead?"

"I want to explain to the judge what happened," I told him.

"You have that right, but the judge could give you up to 12 months in jail and a $2,500 fine," the lawyer said.

"I understand," I said, but I was thinking, *I'd rather take my chances with the judge than with you.* I didn't want to spend *any* time in jail. A month later, I was about to go in front of the judge. Before I stepped into the courtroom, I prayed, "God, you know this situation from the beginning to the end. You know my heart is to help young men. Please be my lawyer in the courtroom. In Jesus name, amen."

As I stood before the judge, the DA told him what he was offering, and my lawyer told the judge that he recommended that I take that deal. Then the judge asked me if I had anything that I would like to say. I explained to him

A Coach's Faith

that I had written the check as a security deposit for the house and that the parents had not paid me all the money I needed to cover the check. He asked me to explain the program and I did. I told him that I didn't write the check with the intention of defrauding the homeowner. He asked if I had kept in touch with the homeowner, and I told him I had. Then he asked me how long the kids had lived in the house. I told him about 30 days. The judge leaned back in his chair and thought for a minute. Then he looked right at me.

"Mr. Freeman," he said, "I commend you for what you are doing with these young men, so here is what we are going to do. Can you pay restitution on the check today?"

"Yes sir, I can," I said.

"Okay," he said, "you pay the restitution today by 5 p.m., and I'll let you go without any fines, probation, or jail time." Then he looked at the DA and said, "I don't see any need for Mr. Freeman to have a felony on his record, do you?" The DA hesitated for a moment, then said, "No, your honor."

Tim Freeman

Then the judge said, "I'm going to reduce your charge from a felony to a misdemeanor."

(I left that courtroom praising God, but in 2008 that check would come back to bite me. At that time, I was working for a friend's car service doing airport transportation. Homeland security was tightening restrictions on transportation services, and everyone who drove had to get a new chauffeur's license, which included a background check. The bad check came up on my record, and I was denied my chauffeur's license. I appealed, but the agency said that the bad check was considered a theft, so I lost my job. I just prayed, "God, when is this circle going to be broken?")

Chapter 9

As I started recruiting for the 2005-2006 season, the first person I had to recruit was a new head coach. I had the perfect person in mind for the job: John Wilkins, a good friend of mine and the old brother of former NBA star Dominique Wilkins. I had spoken with John in the past about our program and knew he had coached an AAU team and trained a number of players. This would be the first time I would speak to him about coaching for me. On the day I was going to have a 7-foot center recruit come in for a visit, I set up a meeting with John to come take look at the gym and classes. I timed it perfectly. As the player and his parents were leaving, John walked into the gym. When John saw the 7-footer, his eyes lit up. When I introduced John as Dominique's brother and possibly our new coach, the whole family's eyes lit up. I got both of the men I wanted.

Coach Wilkins and I went on to recruit a very good team that included Jonathan Belt, a 230-pound 6'7" small forward from Covington, Georgia. Jonathan lived in a group home because his mom had passed away and his father was in prison. He had been living with his grandmother. When Jonathan got into some trouble as a juvenile, the state said that because of his grandmother's poor health, she was not able to care for him, so they placed him in foster care. On the day Jonathan came to try out for the team and visit the school, I met Miss Cindy, who was the group home director and Jonathan's adopted mother. Miss Cindy brought Jonathan's file with her. We knew he was a great athlete, but we were surprised to learn that he was also great student. Jonathan had posted a score of 25 on the ACT. He needed to get a couple of core classes to get him to the NCAA 14 core class he needed to qualify for freshmen eligibility. After looking over his paperwork, I showed Miss Cindy the academic plan that Jonathan would have to follow to get what he would need to gain freshmen eligibility. She liked the plan and agreed to let Jonathan attend our program.

To avoid some of the financial problems we had in the past, I put in place a team fee that would help offset some of our operating costs. Every player we signed that year agreed to pay the fee. About halfway through the first semester, we started to have problems with the players' families paying their fees. The apartments I had them living in were ready to evict them, and I could not make payroll because donations were coming in very slowly. Everyone—coaches, teachers, players, and parents--started to turn against me. I could understand the coaches and teachers being upset. I even understood the anger from those parents who had paid their program fee on time. But what was odd was that the people who were raising the most hell were the ones who had paid nothing.

Miss Cindy called me and told me she wanted to help. She said that after we came back from the Christmas break, we could move the program to Covington at the Group Home campus. They also had an accredited school there where we could hold classes, as well as a gym we could use for practices. Not only that, there were a couple of cabins on their campus she said we could use to house the players. They would be even be able to eat at the cafeteria on campus. I needed to set up a meeting with the president of the AAU program that three of our players came from to see if he could help with funding the program.

On the day of the meeting, he came at me with the most hateful attitude I've ever had directed toward me. He told me I was a bad businessman to have put these kids in this predicament. I showed him my players' commitment letters indicating how much they would pay and signed by the each player and his parents, along with bank account records of where the money went that was paid to the program. During a break in the meeting, Miss Cindy and the AAU president met. When we all came back together, Miss Cindy said she had told the AAU president that she would do what she had told me on the phone. The AAU president said he would let

A Coach's Faith

us use a van to transport the players, and he would pay our coaches for the remainder of the season. Then Mr. President looked at me and said, "I'm going to pay the coaches, but you are on your own." I looked right back at him and said I was fine with that. I asked them if we could still do our Bible class with them. Miss Cindy said that because the Group Home was funded by the state, we could do religious actives on campus. Then Mr. President spoke up and said, "I don't believe in God anyway." That statement summed up his whole attitude. If you ever get a person who doesn't fear God, you have a dangerous person on your hands. Money was his God. That's what he worshipped. He wanted to control things. We agreed that any money that came into the program would go to the Group Home for food, housing, and other expenses. I was satisfied that the program had a home and the players could get what they needed.

At the start of the second semester, there was still a lot of bad feeling directed toward me. But I talked with God, and I said, "God, every year at some point it's just been me and you. It will always be you. As long as I have you, I don't need anybody else." So I went about my business, helping the kids get recruited by colleges. We continued to have coaches from other schools coming to our practices and games. One day I got a call from the father of one of our players. He was an AAU coach. He said one of the kids had called him and complained that they weren't being recruited. I told him I had something to show him and asked that he meet me at the game that night. After the game, I met with him and the players, and I showed him a spreadsheet for who was being recruited by which colleges and recruiting letters from the colleges.

The problem was that several of the players who were being recruited by mid-major Division I colleges such as Georgia State, Southern University, Alabama A&M, and Georgia Southern thought they should be getting recruited by major Division I colleges such as Georgia and Georgia Tech. I explained to them as I had done when I was recruiting them that the major Division I colleges had seen them in high school, at AAU events, and at tournaments we have played

A Coach's Faith

in. "Believe me," I said, "if they wanted you, they would have called you." I told them that recruiting is like dating. If you can't be with the one you love, you'd better be with the one who loves you.

Chapter 10

Everything was going fairly well. The players were okay with living at the group home. And we were winning games. At the end of the season, we played in the national prep school tournament in Jackson, Mississippi, and ended up ranked 6th in the nation. We started having our end-of-season workouts for college coaches to come in and look at our players.

During the second semester as the team was traveling, I was speaking with different coaches and heard a rumor that the NCAA was cracking down on prep schools they called "diploma mills." We knew we were doing the right thing as a program, so I wasn't worried. Our players were going to classes, and we were following the NCAA rules on what kids could do academically in a post-graduate year.

One morning in April 2006, I was as sick as dog, so I did not go to work that day. I got a phone call about 8 a.m.

from the person who ran the group home where our players were staying. He said that when he brought the kids to the cafeteria for breakfast, he saw some strangers standing outside. They told him they were from the NCAA and were there to investigate our program. They said the players could finish their breakfast, after which they were to meet with the investigators at the school. Once the players got to the school, the NCAA officials separated the players, one to a room, and began interrogating them. Normally, I would have come right over, but I had the worst case of the flu I had ever had.

I was confident that we had met all the NCAA requirements. But a month later, the NCAA posted a list on their Web site of schools they would no longer accept classes from, and we were on the list. I hadn't seen the list, but a reporter from the *Washington Post* called me to see if I would be willing to comment on the NCAA's decision. I said I would have no comment. When I got off the phone, I went straight to the Web site to check it out. Two days later, I received letter from the NCAA making it official. They would

A Coach's Faith

no longer accept classes from North Atlanta Prep Academy for freshmen eligibility. I called the lead investigator and asked what we had done wrong. She simply said we needed to hire more teachers. They did not want teachers teaching multiple classes. I told her we would hire more teachers for the upcoming year, and she said they would review our current players' transcripts individually for 2006.

The NCAA eventually cleared all the players who had passed the required classes for freshmen eligibility. At the end of the school year, I met with Miss Cindy about our future plans. She said it would be possible to create a separate sports program for the kids at the group home. But because the group home received state funding, we would not be able to do the Bible classes. So I decided to move our post-graduate program back to Mt. Paran North Church of God.

As I was planning for the 2006-2007 school year, I met with Dr. Ware because it was time for our two-year review with the Georgia Accrediting Commission. I spoke to her and her husband Greg about the problem we had had with the NCAA the year before, and I asked her if she would help me refile the paperwork for the NCAA so they would put our program on their list of schools they would accept classes from. She said she would. Her husband was a successful businessman, so I asked him if he would be our business manager. He agreed. That freed me to focus my attention on the athletic side of things.

Our first step was to hire more teachers. We hired six of them. Dr. Ware met with the accrediting commission, and they approved us for full accreditation. Coach Wilkins and Coach Overall decided to return for 2007. As coach Wilkins and I were recruiting, we put together another dream team. Our top recruits were Jimmy Oden from Tennessee; Chris Hines from Alabama; Britton Smith, a local player; and Hillary Hailey from Washington, D.C. We went through our normal preschool year planning period during June and July, and the players reported on the last weekend in August. This gave us time to get them ready for the fall recruiting period that ran from September through the first week of October. I

A Coach's Faith

really wanted to be able to get the maximum amount of exposure for our program to show everyone we were still here. So I put together a showcase tournament for the last Friday and Saturday in September and called it the Atlanta Prep Classic. I invited three of the top post-grad programs around: Harmony Prep from Cincinnati, The Patterson School from North Carolina, and Covenant Christian from Marietta.

Mt. Paran's gym was very small, with two rollout bleachers that seated 50 people each. We put out about 50 additional chairs behind the home and visitors' benches, and about 25 chairs along the baseline for the college coaches. Hiawatha Betha, a church member who later became our team chaplain and a dear friend, met with each team between games and led a Bible study with the players while they ate lunch. The sports department of the church gave each player a gift bag that included a pocket Bible from the Gideon Society, a tournament T-shirt, and assorted candy. On the day of the tournament, I started receiving phone calls from coaches saying their NCAA compliance officer told them they could not come because the event was not sanctioned by the NCAA. But I had done my homework. I knew that what we were doing was legal under the recruiting rules. So I called an NCAA official and explained what was going on. The NCAA faxed a letter stating that it was okay for the college coaches to attend. That night we had a who's who of college coaches in our gym. When the Ware's got to the gym, they could not believe what they were seeing. It was standing room only. Mr. Ware said, "Boy, I remember when you first mentioned doing this. Everybody thought you were crazy." The Atlanta Prep Classic turned out to be a huge success.

Chapter 11

We moved into November as the regular season got started. The only issue the team had was the uniforms. We wanted to get new uniforms, but the budget would only allow us to buy reversible mesh rather than a heavy-duty fabric. I learned early on that as a program with a small budget you can't afford to spend a lot of money on uniforms when you have other more pressing needs such as salaries, equipment, and travel. Jim Oden's dad called and said he had some uniforms from his AAU team we could use. That solved the uniform issue.

The next issue that arrived going into the Christmas break was the same as in past years: the players' families were not paying their fees on time. Therefore, we were not able to pay the salaries of coaches and teachers on time. Over the Christmas break, Coach Wilkins called and said he and Coach Dunn would not be returning. I met with Mr. Ware, who told me he had someone who would coach the semester for free. I spoke with the parents to let them know about the coaching changes. They were okay with it. At the beginning of the second semester, Coach Keith Lundy took over the program. He was young and energetic. The first day of practice, he challenged the whole team to a three-point shooting contest. He told them to line up single file.

"You're going the shoot the ball and get your own rebound, then pass the ball back to the next man," he said. "I'm going to shoot from this side, and Coach Freeman is going to rebound for me. The first one to hit twenty shots wins." Coach Lundy won the contest 20-16. More important, he won over the team. As far as I was concerned, everything was going along great. We were playing in major prep school tournaments. We had a terrific coach who was willing to work for free. And we had gotten free uniforms. This is the way God works. The year before, Mr. AAU President hated me.

At the beginning of the second semester we did not have enough money to rent a van for away games. So on faith I called up the director of his AAU program and told him our situation and asked if we could borrow the van they let us use the year before. He said he wasn't using it right now, so it wouldn't be a problem for us to use it. Now you have to understand that we did not just take trips

A Coach's Faith

across town. We went to Johnson City, Tennessee, a five-hour drive; Boone, North Carolina, a five-hour drive; and Cincinnati, Ohio, a seven-hour drive; plus our local games. Still, God was answering my prayers and providing.

Chaplain Hiawatha had played a major role during the season, coming by every Wednesday before practice and speaking to the team. He always brought Gatorade with him, and whoever could answer a Bible question from the week before would get a bottle of Gatorade. Naturally, the players nicknamed him "Mr. Gatorade." I believe this group was the most well-rounded group of young men we ever had. Every one of them went on to graduate from a four-year college.

Typically, we would get guys in who were strong in one category or another. For example, we'd have a team that was good academically but couldn't shoot so well. Or we'd have a bunch of gifted athletes who weren't willing to work as hard on their schoolwork. Or we'd have guys who were good athletes and students but were knuckleheads. This year's group was a special one.

On the academic side of things, we had dedicated teachers who were doing a really good job with the players. One of our best teachers, Mr. Dennis, taught our SAT and ACT prep class, and our guys were scoring very well on these tests. Chris Hines, our star player, was being recruited by the most colleges. His senior year of high school he was named Alabama Player of the Year. Chris had had a hard childhood. He came from a large family, the youngest of eight kids, and his parents died when he was in middle school. He bounced around a lot, living with older brothers and sisters, and having to change schools a couple of times. He was very smart, but because of his circumstances his grades were low. He graduated from high school with a 2.0 core GPA and would need to score a 21 on the ACT to qualify for NCAA freshman eligibility. That was going to be tough. The highest ACT score he had attained in high school was a 16. But after working with Mr. Dennis for three months, Chris took the test again and scored a 26. He was ecstatic. But a couple of weeks later, the ACT flagged his score, saying he had made too big of a jump from his previous score. I immediately filed an appeal. They allowed him to retake the test, and this time he scored a 19. You have to score within at least three points of the score that was flagged for the higher score to be upheld. So the score they would accept was a 19, which was two points below what he needed for eligibility. Even so, there were still a number of schools

A Coach's Faith

that were interested in placing him in junior college and getting him in two years after he graduated. Chris ended up going to a junior college and later became a starter for the University of Alabama, which was his dream school.

Our second top recruit in this class was Hillary Haley. Hillary was placed in our program by East Carolina, a major four-year university. Hillary had a low high school GPA and poor test scores. But one thing he had in his favor was that he had a documented learning disability, which meant he could retake the classes in which he made low grades in high school and, if he did better the second time around, replace them on his transcript to raise his core GPA. Because of his disability he could also get the same accommodation on the SAT as he had in the classroom, which in his case meant he could have extra time to take the test. Hillary changed his mind about going to East Carolina because several other schools were interested in recruiting him. Hillary passed the classes he was taking, but did not do well on the SAT. Some of the college coaches asked me how he could be eligible to play next year, and I told them that their school would have to file a disability waiver with the NCAA showing that he tried his best to attain eligibility on his own. Hillary had taken SAT prep classes and had taken the SAT as many times as he could. He had also taken classes to try to raise his GPA but had fallen short. As part of the disability waiver request, a school would have to outline an academic plan for how they would be able to help him graduate. Hillary eventually signed with St. Bonaventure University and played there his freshmen year before transferring to Maryland Eastern Shore University, where he graduated in 2012.

Britton Smith also had learning disability. He signed with The University of Tennessee at Martin. They chose not to file a disability wavier with the NCAA for Britton, instead placing him at East Mississippi Junior College. After two years, he transferred to Mars Hill College in North Carolina. During his junior season, the NCAA ruled him ineligible to play because they said North Atlanta Prep was not certified in 2007, the year he graduated. Britton transferred to Belhaven University, where he graduated in the spring of 2012. The reason I'm telling these young men's stories is that they both had similar circumstances but took two different paths to get the same result: becoming college graduates. They did not let their disabilities hold them back.

Chapter 12

During the second semester of that year, I met with the Wares about my plans for the 2007-2008 year. I had a vision of starting a football program. They thought it was a good idea because it would bring in 45 more students, which would mean more income. I knew we would need to raise money for equipment, so I spoke to Michael Reid, a former Atlanta Falcons player who had been a friend of mine for about 15 years.

When I told him my vision for the program, he agreed that it was something badly needed in the Atlanta area. I told him I wanted start a booster club to raise money and asked him if he would be interested in coaching the team. He said he didn't have the time but had a friend who might be interested. A couple of weeks later, he set up a meeting with Frank Adams, who agreed to be the head coach. Frank was a personal trainer and high school football coach who had been an All-SEC cornerback the University of South Carolina. He had also played a year with the Pittsburgh Steelers and had played Canadian and arena football.

Now that we had a coach in place, we had to start recruiting. I put together a recruiting brochure and started hitting the local high schools. My vision was to find the best 45 players we could within a 30-mile radius of the church who could commute to classes and practices. My plan was to play six to eight games against teams within a four-hour driving distance. We held our first tryout a few weeks later. Out of the two dozen or so kids who showed up, we found twelve who we felt had enough talent to build a team around. About that time, I met with Mike and Mr. Ware to tell them about a $250,000 federal grant that was available for non-profits that had second-chance education programs like ours. I told them to look into it because I would be busy building the program.

One Saturday morning in mid-April, I got a call from the Wares. They wanted me to come to the house to speak

A Coach's Faith

with me. When I got there we sat down at the table, and they said it had been brought to their attention by some of the staff that I was hard to get along with. They told me that Coach Lundy had said I was an arrogant know-it-all who thought that everything had to be done my way. Then they asked me why I would have students who had graduated from high school taking classes. I explained to them that under NCAA rules, kids could retake classes they had done poorly in so they could raise their GPA high enough for Division II freshmen eligibility. The fact that these kids had a high school diploma was irrelevant. I knew where all this had originated. One of our students who was lazy and didn't want to do the work had complained to the Wares. They look at each other then asked me why I hadn't told them about the *Washington Post* article that was on the Internet. I said it was no big deal. I had told them about hold NCAA investigation and had given them all the papers so Dr. Ware could do the paperwork on getting us reproved by the NCAA. Then Mr. Ware said they were going to step away from the program. I said okay. Mr. Ware then abruptly asked me to leave his house.

This really bothered me the entire weekend. I tried to make sense of it but just could not. On my way to work Monday morning I called him and asked if I could meet with him. He said to come by about 6 p.m. When we sat down, I told him I didn't know what the staff was talking about when they said I was arrogant. I thought that the Wares had known me long enough to know that wasn't the truth. Still, I had felt their anger toward me on Saturday. If it turned out that we were going to part ways, I still wanted us to be friends. "I don't want to lose a friendship over a he-said, she-said," I told Mr. and Mrs. Ware as soon as I sat down. They agreed, but they were vague about exactly why they were withdrawing their support. After we parted that evening, I started putting together plans to do the program without them.

About two weeks later, Mr. Ware called and said that he and his wife had been doing some thinking about all this and said they wanted me to come by the house again. This

A Coach's Faith

time they were a little more friendly. We sat down at the table and Mr. Ware said they had been thinking about what I had said the last time I was there. "You're right," he said. "We *are* friends. That's why we want to tell you about the deal we have going on." Mr. Ware said that he and his wife had had some people contact them from overseas about starting a prep school in Atlanta. "We met with them a couple of times to talk about it, and we think it's a great opportunity. But they want it done in a short time. They have some funding for this project, and if you'd like to be a part of this, we may be able to find a position for you because they want to create a big-time sports program to go with it." He told me he was planning to meet with them this weekend and would let me know what they said.

The next week he invited me back and said he had met with the key people, who he said want us to get this prep school started this coming fall. The problem, he said, was that there was not enough time to get all the accreditation, non-profit, and other paperwork done in time. He asked me if I would be willing to sell my prep school to them. "My wife and I would be running the school," he said, "and I would hire you as the athletic coordinator." Then he asked me how much would I take for the accreditation and non-profit status, my Dun & Bradstreet number, and our high school code. Because of the financial difficulty I was having, my first thought was that this might be a way out. Off the top of my head, I said, "Considering all the time and effort I've put into this, I think a fair price would be $40,000." Judging by his facial expression, I immediately knew I should have asked for more.

He said he would let them know and get back with me. A couple of days later he called and told me that his partners said we had a deal. He also said they had agreed to pay me a salary of $45,000 as athletic coordinator. I said okay, but in my spirit I sensed that something was not right. He asked me to get the paperwork to him as soon as possible so he could get things in motion. I said okay, but I was going to need a $5,000 deposit first.

A Coach's Faith

A couple of days later, I dropped off the paperwork and got my check. He said they were having a planning meeting on Saturday morning for the upcoming year and asked if I could be there. He said there were going to be some former staff members there from my prep school from last year who still had some bad feelings toward me. He told me he didn't want there to be any trouble. I said I understood. The meeting went fine, and everything seemed to be going well.

A few days later, Mr. Ware called and asked if I could set up a meeting with my contact at Mt. Paran Church of God about using their classrooms and gym. I had a talk with Lynn Beth, who headed their sports ministry department, and she agreed to meet with them. During the meeting, there was a great deal of tension in the room. Every time I spoke, Mr. Ware would cut me off. He was pressing Lynn Beth for more than I had asked her for. She listened with her arms folded and didn't say much, but I could tell she was getting irritated.

At the end of the meeting, she said she was willing to let them use the classrooms, the gym, and the soccer field for football practice. They shook hands at the end of the meeting, and Mr. Ware left. Lynn Beth invited me to her office and when we got there she said, "Are you *sure* this is what you want to do? I don't have a good feeling about the whole thing." I told her I was sure. Then she said, "If you're sure, I'll support you 100 percent—but I don't like it. The only reason I'm doing this is because of you." When I told Hiawatha, our chaplain, he said almost the same thing as Lynn Beth. He had strong misgivings as well.

Chapter 13

Despite the warnings, I went to work putting together our football coaching staff for the fall. One of the assistant coaches had great recruiting contacts in Georgia, Florida, Alabama, and Tennessee. Because I was no longer the owner and merely the athletic coordinator and offensive line coach, everybody started offering their opinions to Mr. Ware about how things should go. For example, I put together a budget for equipment costs, stadium rental, and travel costs. Other coaches had different ideas. Experience told me we should spend less the first year to minimize financial stress. The other coaches thought we should spend more to look good. When I told Mr. Ware how I thought things should be, he said, "You don't know everything." Then he told me I should humble myself. So that's what I did. Meanwhile, I was thinking, *You just better have my check.* He was supposed pay me the

$35,000 balance over the next six months, and I was depending on him to keep his word.

The first weekend in June we planned to have a one-day football tryout at Mt. Paran so the kids could see the facilities. I asked Mr. Ware what the name of the new school was going to be so I could put together some recruiting materials. He said they had voted at the last meeting to name it Ware Prep Academy. The name didn't matter to him, he said. The only thing he cared about was that the colors would be purple, white, and gold. I thought it was odd that his overseas partners who were putting up the money would allow the school to be named after him. But I let that thought pass. I had bigger fish to fry.

Sixty players showed up for tryouts. Overall, it was a good day. There were about 40 we decided to keep. After the tryouts, we grilled hotdogs and hamburgers for the players. At end of the day, the players left the parking lot a mess. Paper was everywhere. Mr. Ware and all the other coaches had left,

A Coach's Faith

and I was the only one out there picking it up. I began to wonder if this might be a sign of things to come.

In late June we had a meeting with the Wares, who had decided to move the school to Morris Brown College in downtown Atlanta. They said this would allow us to have our own dorms, office space, and classrooms. We would also have use of their gym and football stadium. I pulled Mr. Ware to the side and asked him if he had been to Morris Brown lately. I told him that a friend of mine had considered renting space there for his AAU basketball program. He said it looked like when the school lost its accreditation, they told everyone to go home and left everything where it was.

Student files were in desk drawers, and there was water damage everywhere. The ceilings leaked in the gym and in the classrooms we were going to be using. There was also water damage in the offices and locker rooms in the football stadium. As if that weren't enough, there was structural damage from the vibrations of the MARTA railway tunnel that ran under one end of the stadium. Plus, the officials at Morris Brown were asking way too much for the rent. Mr. Ware simply said, "Tim, the decision's already been made." I said, "Okay," but I was thinking, *You don't know what you're getting into.*

In the last week of August we had a meeting at Morris Brown College with the faculty, coaching staff, and board of directors. To this point I had only worked with the football staff, so this would be my first encounter with the board and the rest of the staff. I was sitting there waiting for the meeting to start when I saw Coach Wilkins, Coach Dunn, Coach Lundy, and all the teachers who had worked with me at my prior prep school walk in. Then the board of directors walked in: Mike Reid and Bobby Taylor, the same people who a year earlier promised to start my booster club.

After the meeting was over, I asked Mr. Ware how he managed to get Coach Wilkins to agree to coach. He said the people who wanted to put the school together had him on board already. When I asked Coach Wilkins the same question, he had a different story. He said Mr. Ware had invited him to a meeting to talk about starting the prep school. I asked him about the overseas investors who were supposed to have brought him in, but he said he knew nothing about them. It was all starting to make sense. I'd been had. I felt a mix of anger, fear, and hurt. At that moment, I doubted whether I would see that $35,000 materialize. But I didn't say anything.

A few weeks went by. One day Mr. Ware came by the school and said he and the board of directors had had a meeting with the investors about a $250,000 grant they we close to getting. It wasn't until I got home later that I put it all together. The grant he was talking about was the same $250,000 grant I had told him about in March. He had screwed me out of the program I had worked so hard for so he could secure that grant for his own school.

I was madder than I had ever been. I didn't know what do. I remember lying on the floor crying, repeating over and over again, "I love God. I love Jesus. Walk by faith, not by sight. No enemy formed against me shall prosper. The

Lord will make my enemy my footstool." After that night, every time I saw Mr. Ware or thought of him, I started repeating this to myself.

After the first month of the school year, we had money problems. We had to cancel a couple football games because we didn't have money for the bus. The school wasn't able to make payroll, and some of the coaches and teachers quit. I decided to stay through the football season even though Mr. Ware was only giving me about a third of my salary. We wound up playing five football games. The beginning of the end of the football program came when we were supposed to go to Valdosta to play the final game of the season. We met at the stadium, but the bus didn't show up because Mr. Ware hadn't paid them. I had to tell the players we were going to have to cancel the game. Naturally, they were upset. After that, I held on for another week before I finally quit. The school closed down for good just before Christmas.

All of this was learning experience for me. Whenever you're doing God's work, you have to have likeminded

A Coach's Faith

people around you. The Bible warns us to look out for false prophets. There were, of course, some good things that happened along the way. I was able to help a few players get into Junior college: Jarvis Blue, Louisburg College; Jeffery Harris, Louisburg College/Alabama State; Wesley Journey, Louisburg College/Benedict College; Johnnie Lee Dixon, Peal River Community College/Canadian Football League; Bruce Irvin, Butler Community College/University of West Virginia/Seattle Seahawks; and DeMarlo Belcher, Indiana University.

Chapter 14

Living on a partial salary had only worsened my financial problems. I was two months behind on my rent. Luckily I had an understanding landlord who allowed me to make payments when I could. During my time at Ware Prep, I had also been working part-time at my friend Mark's car service doing airport pick-ups and drop-offs. After I quit the school, I started working full-time for Mark trying to make ends meet. During the times I was waiting for a pick-up at the airport, I would pray and meditate that God would restore my vision and reveal his will for my life.

In January 2008 I started doing early morning pick-ups. I would leave home at 5:45 a.m., and I began listening to comedian Steve Harvey's morning show. Every morning Steve would come on and say, "Steve got a radio show." Then he would give his morning inspiration. Soon, I started every morning by saying, "Tim Freeman got a football program." I started getting a vision of how to do a new prep program. Every day I would bring a notebook to work with me. Whenever I had down time, I would just write out my vision as God gave it to me.

In 2008 God really set me up for a change in my life. Because of my financial problems, my family and I had to move from our home. This was the third time in eight years we had had to move. But this time was different. In the past I felt like a failure and would go into a depressed state. This time I like I felt like I wasn't losing anything but gaining. I took the attitude that I had already lost everything. That was behind me. Now, everything was there for me to gain. Just as Job lost everything and because of his faith God multiplied what he had tenfold, I was now looking for my Job blessing.

My friend Mark suggested that I move closer to where he lived so I wouldn't have to travel so far to pick up my car for work. I had remembered turning around in a driveway of a house in a neighborhood not too far away from

A Coach's Faith

where he lived that was for rent. We went out and looked for a house to rent and found one. I was nervous about telling the landlord my financial history. But I told him on faith about why we had to move and that I was working with Mark. He told me the rent was $1,600. Then he asked me how much could I afford. Mark told the landlord that we could do $1,100 and that he would make sure I had it. It turned out the landlord was a pastor who wanted to help people get back on their feet.

I went back and told Melanie about the house that Mark and I had found. I asked her how she felt about the move. She said, "I know you've had jobs doing whatever you could do to support our family, but just when we get out of a rut, something always happens and we are right back where we started. For the longest time, I have misplaced my anger about our hardships. I've been blaming God when in reality he was the glue that held us together. He's the one who has never left our side. He's seen us through everything. He gave us breath when we didn't feel strong enough to breathe for ourselves. As for this next move, all we can do is trust Him."

Tim Freeman

We waited until the end of the school year to move, so we didn't have to take the kids out of school.

So now I would be able to do my own program this year because I still wanted to coach. I volunteered to coach the Northside Christian Association Lions (NCA Lions), who were the very first group in the county to do a football team for home-schooled high school students. This was a challenge for several reasons. One was that I was used to coaching players with college-level talent. The Northside program was on the decline because new programs in the area that had more money were pulling players away. When I agreed to coach the team in April 2008, we had three players returning from the year before. I had to go around all the home-school groups and recruit players. By June, I had 18 players: three returning from the year before, seven who had played at least one year of youth league football, and eight who had never played football before. Tim Freeman got a football team.

I went to Coach Frank, who had coached with me at Ware Prep. Frank is a personal trainer with his own gym. I

A Coach's Faith

asked him if he would be willing to train the team for one hour a day three times a week to help me get them in shape for the summer. He agreed. I watched the kids work out as often as I could, and I could see that the kids and their parents were dedicated to the program. I got new uniforms and had our blue helmets painted gold to change the attitude of the team. When we started practice to get ready for the season, I had to begin with the basics because most of the players had a very low football IQ and skill level. All we worked on was how to block and tackle and a handful of plays.

The first game of the season we played the defending league champs. They beat us 56-0, but I saw something in my players that I hadn't seen in a long time: a genuine love for football. It didn't matter to them that they lost. All that mattered to them was that they were playing football. We went on to lose every game that season. The last game of the season it rained the entire game, and we lost 56-0 just like the first game of the season. At the end of the game, our players and the players from the other team were running and sliding in a giant mud puddle on the field. Even though we had lost every game of the season and there was no college scholarship ahead for these kids, they were still holding their heads up. This was in stark contrast to my experience with prep school and junior college players, who had a lot more talent but also had a lot more ego. They tended to only focus on themselves and what they were going to get out of the program. What I had here was a bunch of kids who were all about team.

I could see why God had brought me here. Despite the losing, this season was fun for me because I learned to use the game as a way to teach kids not only the basics of football but of life. In life, I taught them, even though you may lose the game, what really matters is that you played. You may have a losing season, but just as a coach evaluates the game film to see where the team needs to get better, we need to reevaluate our life game plan each week to see what changes we need to make.

Chapter 15

I knew in 2009 that I was going to going to start a new prep program. God had given me the vision. Because the new NCAA rules said that a prep school player could only put one core class back on their high school transcript, or three core classes if they had a learning disability, I decided that we would use junior college rules, which would make things a lot simpler for us.

Under the rules of the National Junior College Athletic Association (NJCAA), a player transferring to an NCAA Division 1 school would have to graduate with a 2.5 GPA and an associate's degree. A player transferring to an NCAA Division II school would have to have 48 transferable credits. For NCAA Division III or NAIA would need 36 transferable credits. If a player was a full NCAA Division 1 qualifier, he would only need 12 transferable credits in a semester. What all this meant was that I wouldn't have to hire a teaching staff and jump through a lot of hoops. It would also allow us to send our players to Chattahoochee Technical College or North Metro, whichever was closer to where they lived so they could commute to take their academic classes.

In February 2009, I assembled the coaching staff, most of whom had been on my staff at Ware Prep. One of them was Coach Marino, who would be our head coach. Another was Coach Deveren, who would be our offensive coordinator. And finally Coach Frank, who would be our strength and conditioning coach. I also hired Erasmus Harvey, who I had met at a tryout we had, to be our defensive coordinator. Coach Harvey operated a recruiting service as well as strength and conditioning business. Hiawatha, who had led Bible classes at Ware Prep, agreed to do the same for us. My title was director, but I also did some coaching as needed. We immediately started holding tryouts to find the 45 best players we could. I made arrangements for the players who were going to be part of our program who lived outside

A Coach's Faith

of commuting distance to live at Garrison Lake Apartments, which was walking distance from the Chattahoochee Tech campus. Each player would have to pay a $2,500 fee to be a part the team. The good thing about these kids going to Chattahoochee Tech was that they would automatically qualify to receive Georgia's HOPE grant, which at the time paid 100 percent of their tuition.

We held an open house at Mt. Paran, which now was our base of operation. The first part of the day was orientation, and I had recruiters there from the Chattahoochee Tech and North Metro campuses. The recruiter from North Metro was David Archer Jr., who I knew from prep school basketball. He had directed and coached the Summer Hill Prep program. Coach Archer had been hired by North Metro as their head club basketball coach, athletic coordinator, and admissions recruiter. The open house went great. We got every single player we went after. When it was almost time for school to start, the players had to meet with their academic advisors to get their class schedules. One day at practice a player gave me a note with a phone number on it and said his advisor was Ms. Tillman, the cheerleading coach at Chattahoochee Tech. She wanted me to call her to see about having the girls cheer at our home games. I called and told her about the program and what we were trying to accomplish. She explained that her team was a competition cheerleading team and that she would love to have them cheer for us to stay active during their off-season. It was perfect fit. Having cheerleaders would add a lot of spirit to our games. Soon after that, we had a meet and greet with our players and the cheerleaders, which created a bond between us and the school. We got everyone settled in by the first week of August and held our first practice. The first week of practice we had two-a-days. In the morning, Coach Frank did a boot camp conditioning workout with the players, and in the afternoon we held a regular practice.

Things were going smoothly for the first four weeks. Then some problems started to emerge. The main one was that some of the parents had fallen behind on paying their fees, and money was running low. We had a trip scheduled to

A Coach's Faith

Rome, Georgia, to play Shorter University's JV team. The Thursday before the trip, the owner of the bus company called me and asked if we still needed to go to Rome on Monday. I told him we didn't have the money, so we might have to cancel. "That's not what I asked you," he said. "Don't you *need* to go to Rome?" I said yes, and he said he would have a bus at the regular pick-up spot at 2 p.m. on Monday. "You can pay me when you collect," he said. I told him I would. I knew God was with me. The weekend before the game, it rained cats and dogs. On Monday I got call from the Shorter coach, telling me that the field we were going play on was flooded and that they had cancelled the game.

The next week we played in Valdosta. We were to kick off at 6 p.m., but because of lighting strike within two miles of the stadium, the game was delayed. We finally got to kick off at 8 p.m., so we didn't get back on the bus until 11 p.m. and had a four-hour trip ahead of us. On the way home it rained harder than I had ever seen. Players were calling their families on the phone, and a couple of them found out that

Tim Freeman

their houses had been flooded. We finally got home at 4 a.m. Because of all the flooding in the area, our next two games were cancelled. Our final game was supposed to be against a team from the North Carolina coast, but that area was hit by a major storm, so they had to cancel. To help keep up player morale and confidence in the program, I called around and got us a game with Jirah Prep from Charlotte. About halfway through the third quarter, a fight broke out and both benches cleared. We finally got order restored, and the game went on. It was a Sunday afternoon, and I had a very important meeting I had to attend at 6 p.m. I left the game at the beginning of the fourth quarter. As I was leaving, I called the Acworth police and told them that there had been a fight during the game. I asked them to send an officer to make sure there would be no problems. About 6:40 p.m. I got call from the team chaplain, who told me that at the end of the game the police sent both team to their dressing rooms and were going to let the visiting players dress and leave. Once the visitors were gone, the police were going to let our guys leave. But there was a

A Coach's Faith

breakdown in communication, and the police let our players out of our dressing room too early. A fight ensued in the parking lot between our guys and the visitors, and the police ended up pepper-spraying a couple of people, including Hiawatha. It was a big mess.

The next morning, the Acworth police chief and the head of public safety at Chattahoochee Tech happened to be at a meeting together.

"I heard your football team got into a fight yesterday," the police chief said.

"We don't *have* a football team," the public safety officer replied.

"Well, there was a football team that got into a fight at North Cobb High School, and I was told they were from Chattahoochee Tech."

The head of public safety called the vice president of the school to see if Chattahoochee Tech had a football team. Then the vice president of the school called David Archer, the athletic coordinator. Coach Archer assured him that

Tim Freeman

Chattahoochee Tech did not have a football team, but then he added that there was a local prep program whose players attended Chattahoochee Tech and that Chattahoochee Tech's cheerleaders performed at their games. The vice president told Coach Archer that the college did not want to have anything further to do with our programs. Coach Archer called me that afternoon and told me what the vice president had said. I told him I was sorry about what had happened. I felt terrible, and I thought it was over for the program. I called Hiawatha and told him what was going on, and we prayed that God would give us peace about the situation. The next morning I got a call around 7 a.m. I saw that it was Coach Archer, but I didn't answer because I knew he was more of an email and text type of person. I figured that if he was calling, it couldn't be good. I turned to my wife and said, "I hope I didn't get that man fired." She convinced me to call him back. When I did, he said, "You're not going to believe what happened yesterday."

"Don't tell me you got fired," I said.

A Coach's Faith

"No," he said, "but the president of the college heard about what happened and came looking for me." I didn't know what was coming next. He went on. "I told him about your program, and he wants to meet with you about partnering with the college." I was shocked. I told Melanie what Coach Archer had said, and, of course, she was thrilled. After I got off the phone with Coach Archer, I called Hiawatha and told him the good news. Hiawatha calmly replied, "You see, what man meant for bad, God meant for good." Then he said, "Tim, just think about all the years you've been hoping that someone would notice your program--and it took a fight to make it happen."

Chapter 16

A couple of weeks later, Hiawatha and I scheduled a meeting with the president of Chattahoochee Tech. I wanted Hiawatha with me because I felt I needed a little more Jesus with me than I had on my own. When we got to the meeting room, the president's secretary came in and said her boss was running a few minutes late because of a dental appointment. She brought us some water, and while we were waiting I surveyed the room. We were seated at a huge conference table with about twenty high-backed chairs around it. Coach Archer was there, along with John Furman, the sports information director. I had never been in a setting like this before, and I was a bit intimidated. Here I was, a simple guy just trying to help kids, about to meet with the president of the largest technical college in the state. For the next fifteen minutes we tried to make small talk while we were waiting for the president. It felt like an eternity. Finally, the president walked in and introduced himself.

"I heard you boys had a fight," he said in a deep southern drawl.

"Yes, sir, we did," I replied.

"Well, I like a good fight," he said. "That shows you care about what you're doing when you're willing to fight for it." That broke the ice. I was able to relax. This was someone I could relate to. I was expecting a sophisticated guy with wire-rimmed glasses, a three-piece suit, and a snobby attitude. Instead, he was a simple country boy in a suit.

He looked over my proposal and asked me some questions over the next thirty minutes. Then he sat back in his chair and said, "I believe we can do this." I could tell he was excited. "I have the authority to approve this," he said, "but let me talk to some people downtown and the board members of the college." Then he smiled at me and said, "In the meantime, just go ahead and get started with what you need to do. If anybody asks what you're doing, just tell them you left a football on the field and before you knew it, guys started playing."

I left the meeting feeling pretty good about what was to come.

In January 2010 Dr. Chandler asked me to meet with Coach Archer and Dr. Ron Dulaney, the provost who was over the athletic department, to show them the business plan for the football program. Then in March, all of us got together for a meeting with Dr. Chandler. His secretary asked me to bring my resume to this meeting. During the meeting, I showed everyone the game schedule I had made for the fall. I had gone ahead and schedule these games because I was determined to somehow do the program, even if Chattahoochee Tech turned it down. When Dr. Chandler saw the schedule, his face lit up. "We're going to do this!" he said emphatically. Because this was a state college, I had to ask him if Hiawatha and I could do a weekly Bible study with the players. "You do whatever you see fit to help build young men," he said. "I only have one rule: If you don't pass, you don't play." He asked me what kind of work I was doing. I told him I was selling roofing. He said he would see if he could get me a job at the school. I told him I had applied for a job as the CPR instructor because that was what I did with the fire department. The plan was for us to operate as a club program for two years and then transition to a full National Junior College program. In April we held our first meeting at the college for students who might be interested in our program. About 40 students showed up, and we elected the board for the club team.

Two weeks later, we held tryouts to fill 45 roster spots. A couple of months later, the school hired me to do two jobs in addition to coaching. One was CPR instructor, the other was Employment Readiness Specialist, which meant I would teach life skills, resume-writing, interviewing skills, and time management to people who were trying to get back into the workforce. After nine years of struggling, I was finally going to get a paycheck for what I love to do: help people. Glory be to God!

A Coach's Faith

The athletic and marketing departments of the college did a great job of generating support for our program, including getting a couple of newspaper articles in the local papers. I also got to speak at a kickoff dinner for a rotary club. This wasn't the vision I dreamed of. In my vision, I owned the school. But I knew this was God's will.

I Googled some other club programs to see how they operated and who they played. I came across the National Club Football Association (NCFA), did some research on them, and then spoke with Coach Archer and Dr. Dulaney about joining this league. They thought it would be an excellent opportunity because they did a weekly Top 10 and crowned a national champion at the end of the season. In addition, our players would be eligible to be voted player of the week for the league, which would give the players an extra incentive.

At the end of our third week of training camp, we played our blue vs. white scrimmage. Unfortunately, we didn't receive our equipment until the week of the scrimmage, so our players had not had much time to get used to playing in full pads. As a result, the scrimmage wasn't pretty, but it was productive. Still, I could see that we had a lot of work to do. The next week we played a scrimmage game against the Elite Performers Sports Academy Cobras, which was a first-year prep program owned by Coach Harvey, one of my former coaches. We lost 51-6, but our guys were starting to get their legs, and their football conditioning was getting better.

Our first official game of the season was against Shorter University's JV team on Labor Day evening in Rome, Georgia. Before the game I could see that our mindset wasn't right. The first thing that went bad was that one of our guys tried to drive up to the field using a walkway that wasn't meant for cars. When he tried to back down the walkway, he ran off into a ditch. During pre-game warm-ups our guys weren't running, they were walking. I looked over to the sideline and saw that half of them were sitting on the bench drinking water. I marched them into the end zone and gave

A Coach's Faith

them a good old-fashioned talking to. At halftime I was trying to pinpoint the problem. Then it hit me. When we kicked off at 6 p.m., it was very hot. Our guys were used to practicing at 7 a.m. and being done by 9:30 a.m. They weren't used to the heat. A number of them were cramping up. I told them to relax because the sun had gone down, and it was going to be a lot cooler in the second half. "We're in our element now," I said. "And they're gonna be in big trouble." My speech must have worked because we won 18-6, the first win in the program's history. After the game, parents and fans were coming over to congratulate us on the win. I heard someone behind me say congratulations, and when I turned around, I saw that it was Dr. Chandler. He shook my hand and gave me a hug. I could see the pride in his eyes.

After starting the season 2-0 we entered the NCFA coaches Top 10 poll at Number 9. We won our third game of the season and jumped from Number 9 to Number 5. I was as excited as the kids, but I told them not to let the ranking go to their heads because we had a tough stretch of games ahead. I

Tim Freeman

don't know if they believed me at the time, but we proceeded to lose our next four games. We eventually were able to get it together and win our last game of the season 42-0 over Clemson's club team, finishing with a 4-4 record and a Number 7 ranking in the coaches' poll. As a coach, I would have liked to have won more games, but finishing .500 in our first year was a major accomplishment.

Chapter 17

As we began to recruit for the 2011 season, we wanted to recruit more kids straight out of high school because all they knew was school and football. In contrast, many members of our first-year team were 21 or older and had been out of school for a few years. They had many of the same adult responsibilities as the coaching staff, such as rent, car payments, and in some cases, kids. But unlike the coaches, they hadn't developed good time-management skills, so when life happened, they ended up missing a lot of practice time, and a few had to quit the team. This year, in addition to holding open tryouts, our coaching staff went to recruiting fairs and visited high schools. Because our program was a non-scholarship program, we had to be careful to find kids who had a support system in place—either a family or other people who would make sure they were able to pay their rent and get food on their own. I knew from experience that when kids didn't have a support system, they were more susceptible to the temptation to do wrong when they didn't have the money to pay their bills or buy food.

When building a team, I've always believed in building from the ball out, which means my main priority is to recruit offensive linemen and quarterbacks. In our second year, we were able to recruit three All-State quarterbacks, but offensive linemen were a bit harder to come by. In June 2011, Coach Sandy Stephen and I went to Chattanooga to watch three players we had already signed play in the Tennessee-Georgia high school all-star game. It turned out to be a recruiting trip because we're able to sign three players from the Georgia team who were unsigned: a running back/linebacker named John Hampton, who made first team all-state on offense and defense; Paul Walton, an all-region running back; and Randy Holt, a 6'6" 330-pound offensive lineman who was named the game's offensive MVP. Then a week later, I got an email from a parent about his son, an all-

A Coach's Faith

region player named Craig Rolland, who was looking for somewhere to play. This kid was 6'7" and 315 pounds. I was thinking that with him and Randy at the tackles, we were going be great.

The players reported for summer school the first Saturday in July. I had a three-session plan laid out for our preseason. Session1 was three weeks of strength and conditioning. Session 2 was three weeks of training camp leading to our scrimmage against Georgia Military College. Session 3 was three weeks of game preparation to get ready for our first regular season game. In our team orientation session—also known as my coming to Jesus meeting—I laid out the team rules. I had a special guest speaker come talk to the team.

John Valentine was a high school star football player at Cherokee High School who had secured a scholarship to play at Union College in Kentucky. On his graduation night, he was at a party with his friends and had gotten so drunk that he dove into the shallow end of the swimming pool and hit his head on the bottom, breaking his neck. He was paralyzed from the neck down. He told the team not to take life for granted because before the accident, he thought he was invincible. He told them that the Lord had given him the opportunity to let young people know the dangers of alcohol and drugs. Looking around the room at the faces of these students, I think the talk got through to them.

The next day we held our first practice. The players worked very hard and the coaching staff was very pleased with what we saw. The next morning I noticed that Craig Rolland wasn't at practice and he had not called me. I called him after practice but got no answer. He didn't show up the next morning, either. I asked the players if they had they seen him, and one of them said he had been in class yesterday afternoon. After practice I got a call from Craig, who said he needed to talk with me. We met that afternoon at my office.

"Coach," he said. "I don't want to play football. I *never* wanted to play, but because I was big, my dad *made* me play.

A Coach's Faith

"If you didn't want to play, why are you so good?" I asked him.

"If I had to play," he said, "I wasn't going to let people just run over me. So I took my frustration out on other players."

"In all my years of coaching," I told him, "one thing I've learned is that if a player didn't want to play, don't try to make him." Still, I wanted to leave the door open for him. "If you change your mind in the next couple of days, let me know. And if you ever need to just come by and talk, I'm here." Then I wished him good luck and he left. I never heard from him again.

At the beginning of our second preseason session, we had 12 players report to the team that had to take care of academic problems from their high school or had a transfer issue that needed to be resolved. When they reported, they had to go through a week of conditioning with Coach Matt, who was new to our staff. The plan was for Coach Matt to be a volunteer and learn from Coach Johnson, our receivers coach. The first day of the second week of the second session the new guys got their pads. In this group we had transfers from North Carolina State, the Citadel, Alabama State, and Valdosta State. They were used to having big locker rooms and team managers waiting on them hand and foot. They got a reality check when I told them to meet me at the utility shed by the concession stand to get their equipment. When Coach Evans pulled up the metal door and they saw our equipment stored in a 12-foot by 10-foot room along with the equipment for the rec team we shared the park with, the look on their faces was priceless. They didn't say anything, but they looked at each other like WHAAAAT?!?

After the initial shock wore off, they started to crack jokes and have fun with it. Now we had everyone in full pads and were ready to get down to the business of preparing for our scrimmage with Georgia Military. The next day during a team half-speed drill, one of our defensive linemen hit our quarterback so hard that the quarterback started throwing up. Then he turned around and said to the guy who hit him, "You

A Coach's Faith

gave me a concussion." We sent the injured player to see the trainer, who confirmed that he actually did have a concussion. It was strange to me that the quarterback knew he had a concussion as soon as he got hit, but I later learned that this was his fourth concussion. He had had three in high school. The team doctor told me he wasn't going to clear him to play football ever again.

We were now down to two all-state quarterbacks and a kid who had not played quarterback since 10th grade. That Saturday, we had our scrimmage with GMC, and our team did surprisingly well against one of the top junior college programs in the country. The week after the scrimmage, our all-state quarterback came to see me.

"Coach," he said, "I need to talk to you." I closed the door and asked him to sit down.

"What's going on?" I asked him.

"I've decided to quit the team," he said nervously.

"Why?"

"Football's just not fun for me anymore."

"Are you sure about this?"

"Yes." He went on to explain to me his dad was sick and unable to work. "I need to get a job to help my mom."

I told him the same thing I told Craig. I asked him again if he was sure this was what he wanted, and he said it was. I wished him good luck and that was that. Now we were down to one all-state quarterback and one kid with very little experience, and we only had three weeks to get ready for our season opener. The all-state quarterback we had remaining missed the first day of practice in session three. I said to myself, *Lord I've seen this movie before, and I already know how it ends. Lord, let your will be done.*

This kid, however, was an unbelievable athlete. When I first met him, he was working at the Wal-mart by my house. Another kid who worked there, a friend of my daughter, was going to try out for the team. One day, my daughter and I were in the store and she introduced me to both of them. Christian Clay told me he had played quarterback at a high school in Florida and was all-state his senior year. I

A Coach's Faith

asked him why he wasn't in school, and he said he had graduated in 2010 and had attended a small college in Iowa for a semester but didn't like it, so he moved to Georgia to live with his dad. He suggested I go look him up on YouTube and watch his high school highlights.

I went home, and as soon as I got in the house, I Googled his name. A ton of information came up on him. Then I watched his highlight video, and I couldn't believe how good he was. I called our assistant coach who help me with recruiting and had him watch it. He said all the coaches needed to start going to the nearest Wal-mart right now to recruit. I got back in my van and drove back to Wal-mart. I walk up to Christian and said, "That better be you on that video because if it's not you, I'm going run you until you can't stand up." When I got him out on the practice field, I could tell the talent was still there and he was just was a little rusty.

That Saturday morning Christian called me.

"Coach, I have to go to work today, but I need to talk to you. Can I come by your house tonight when I get off work?"

"Sure," I said. *Here we go again*, I thought to myself. When he came over, I met him on my driveway.

"I need to let you know what's going on with me," he said. "I have a 2-year-old daughter in Florida who's living with my mother. My mother is making me join the military to earn more money to help take care of them. So, I'm not going to be able to play anymore."

So now we've lost three all-state quarterbacks and are down to one quarterback with almost no experience, and only one week to get him ready for our first game. At our first practice that week, we did everything we could to get Reid, our only quarterback, as many reps as possible. This was a big day because at noon the preseason NCFA coaches' poll was coming out, and we held our pre-season media day. At noon, I got an email from the NCFA saying they had us ranked Number 7 in the country, the same place we finished

A Coach's Faith

in 2010. We had reporters there from all the local newspaper in the five counties our school serviced. The marketing department had done an excellent job of setting up the event. Dr. Chandler, our president, spoke about the importance of having athletics at the college. He also talked about how God had brought us together. Then I spoke about the program and gave an overview of the upcoming season, after which I did an interview with a reporter from the Bartow County newspaper that was doing a story on the five players who came from Bartow County. He asked me about Brian Owens, who had played at Cass High School and graduated in 2009. I told him Brian was doing great for us as a slot receiver.

"You know he was an excellent quarterback in high school, don't you?" he asked me with a puzzled look on his face. "Do you think he'll see any action at quarterback this season?"

"Possibly," I said, trying to be cool. I didn't know Brian had played quarterback. The coach who sent him to us

Tim Freeman

had told me he played running back and receiver. After the interview, I walked over to Brian.

"You played quarterback in high school?" I asked him.

"Yes, sir."

"What type of offense did you run?"

"Wing T." I knew he had to be fast to run the Wing T.

"Get your mind right," I told him. "Tomorrow we're going to try you quarterback."

"I got you, Coach," he said confidently, which scared me because any time a kid said that to me he would always let me down. The next morning, Reid, our inexperienced and only remaining quarterback, called and said his grandmother was sick and he had to go out of town. It was God's work to put me in front that reporter the day before. Otherwise, we would have been without a quarterback at practice. On Brian's first play from scrimmage, he called the play that was sent in, read the defense, and sensed that the play wasn't

A Coach's Faith

going to work. So he checked off to another play and threw a touchdown pass. Perfect! I immediately told our offensive coordinator to go through our playbook and find ten plays that fit Brian's skill set. I decided he was going to start on Monday, even though we only had three days of practice to get ready.

Chapter 18

Our first game was on Labor Day, and kickoff was at 6:30 p.m. I went through my regular game routine, which included loading my van and making sure we had all our uniforms and sideline equipment. I was watching the 12 o'clock news to check the weather, and they said severe thunderstorms were heading our way. I monitored the Weather Channel all afternoon. I was back and forth on the phone with the head coach from Point University, our opponent, and the stadium caretaker at Osborne High School where we were playing.

At about 3:30 p.m. we made the decision to play the game, and I left home and headed to the stadium. On the way, I got a phone call from Coach Stephens, one of our assistant coaches, who said that he and his family were in the basement because a tornado had hit his subdivision. He told me he would be at the game as soon as he could. When I got to the stadium, there was a report of a tornado touching down about five miles from the stadium. We decided to start the game a half hour early while there was a break in the weather.

Brian had an excellent first game. His first touchdown came on a fluke play. We were on the five-yard line, and he handed the ball to his running back, who ran into a wall, causing the ball to pop out. It bounced once and landed right in Brian's hands, who then ran around left end for the score. Despite the bad weather, it was clear to me that the ball was literally bouncing our way. Brian ran for another touchdown, and we won 38-6.

The following Wednesday the first regular season NCFA coaches' poll came out. The University of New Orleans was ranked Number 1. There were a couple of teams who had been ranked ahead of us that lost, so we moved up to Number 6. The next morning, I was told by one of the players that their apartment door had been kicked in and that someone had stolen their video games and 52-inch flat-screen TV. I knew that a couple of weeks earlier some other players

A Coach's Faith

had had their apartment broken into, but they lived in a different apartment complex five miles away from this player's apartment. Then a couple of players spoke up and said their apartment had been broken into during the GMC scrimmage. Our coaches got together and figured out that someone much be watching the football players and knew their daily schedule, which meant the thieves knew when the players wouldn't be at home.

I had told the players at the beginning of the season not to let people in their apartments to hang out or spend the night. I said, "When you let people into your apartment, you let them into your world. You're letting them see what you have, and you set yourself up to be taken advantage of by the wrong kind people." After I learned of these three break-ins, I repeated the same warning. Then we went on with our business of getting ready to play Shorter University's JV. On this game day, we had great weather. We played a good all-around game and won 33-6.

Tim Freeman

The Week 2 coaches' poll came out, and we had moved up to Number 5. We were slowly making our way to the top. Thursday evening I got a call from one of the players who thought he had seen his video game on Craigslist. He had called the number on the ad, and a white guy had answered and said he lived in one of the apartments on the other side of campus. Then to add fuel to the fire, a girlfriend of one of our players said that one of the basketball players who lived in the same apartment building had said there was a white guy there who was trying to sell a big-screen TV earlier that day. Our players thought it might have been a former player and his brother who were kicked off the team. A dozen of our players went over to the suspect's apartment to take their stuff back. By the time I arrived, the police were there and our players were gone. Coach Hailey and I explained to the police what was going on. While we were talking, I spotted the ex-player, his brother, their mother, and a friend rushing to load up an SUV like they were trying to get out of town. As they were pulling away, the police stopped them. The officers called in

A Coach's Faith

the detectives who had been investigating the break-ins, and they searched the vehicle and apartment but found nothing. The next morning at practice I told our guys to never try and take the law into their own hands. I explained to them that because they were all over 18, they would likely end up getting themselves in serious trouble, and it would eventually hurt them when they tried to get jobs.

Our third game of the season was a barn burner against Orangeburg-Calhoun Tech, a junior college club team from South Carolina. They played us to double-overtime, and we pulled the game out on a field-goal, 23-20. The Week 3 coaches' poll now had us at Number 2. The next week we would be playing the Columbus State University club team, which we thought would be a challenging game, so we had a tough week of practice leading up to the game. I had underestimated our opponent the week before, and I wanted to make sure I didn't do it again. But we won easily, 40-0.

We were 4-0, and when the Week 4 rankings came out, they had us at Number 1. The only thing that overshadowed our ranking was that one of our players whose apartment been broken into a couple of weeks earlier happened to be visiting another player's apartment and felt something hard poking him when he sat on the couch. When he looked under the cushion, he saw the video game that had been stolen from his apartment. He left and called the police, who searched the apartment and found a lot of the items that had been stolen from other players. The police let the players identify their belongings and retrieve them. The police took the guilty player to jail for receiving stolen goods. I told our players that when he eventually gets out of jail, I didn't want to hear of anyone trying to get revenge. I told them that in the Lord's Prayer, it says, "Forgive us our trespasses as we forgive those who trespass against us." I explained to them that it means that if you want the Lord to forgive you, you're going to have to learn to forgive others. Despite this distraction, the coaching staff and I tried to keep the team as focused on football as possible. The following Sunday we

A Coach's Faith

beat Birmingham Southern's JV 26-10 to go to 5-0 on the season, and I got my first ever Gatorade bath.

Chapter 19

At the beginning of week 5, I met with the coaching staff and told them that coaching a Number 1-ranked team was going to be harder than coaching a Number 7, a Number 5, or a Number 2 team had been. Our biggest challenge was going to be making sure the players stayed grounded. Most of all, I said, we as coaches would have to stay grounded and focused. I reminded them what I had told them at the first coaches' meeting at the beginning of the season—that we as a coaching staff had to be "a team within the team." We all had to be on the same page at all times. If we weren't, the players would pick up on it. I emphasized that now that we were Number 1, we needed to keep doing the things that got us to 5-0.

The coming week we were to play Valdosta State's JV team, one of the best Division II programs in the country. They beat us 13-0 in 2010, but we had only dressed out 28 players for that game. We felt that this time, going into the game with full roster of 53 players, we had a chance to beat them. Unfortunately, we turned the ball over five times, twice inside their five-yard line, and they were able capitalize on the turnovers and beat us 41-12. We also lost one of our starting running backs with a neck injury.

When the Week 6 coaches' poll came out, everyone was nervous, figuring that with the loss we would lose our Number 1 ranking. But we didn't. I couldn't explain it, and I didn't try. The next we week we had another tough road game coming up with Gray Military Academy out of Columbia, South Carolina, at Benedict College Stadium.

When we pulled into the parking lot and saw a big, beautiful new stadium, our players got excited. We noticed that there were fans in the parking lot tailgating. When the bus passed them by, we realized they were our fans, which made us feel good. We were happy to see that they had driven three and a half hours to support our program. When we pulled up

A Coach's Faith

to the field house, I went over to talk to the other team's coach to see where our locker room was going to be.

The coach told me that Benedict College Stadium had two locker rooms, but the college would only let them use one. What this meant was that his team was going to use the visitors' locker, and we would have to dress in the bathrooms at the top of the stadium. I went back and told the bus driver to pull around to the other side of the stadium. I told our guys not to worry about where we were going to have to dress but to enjoy where they would be playing and focus on the game. I called for our special teams players to go out for pregame warm-up, but our top running back wasn't dressed. I told him he had five minutes to get ready or I wasn't going to let him play. When I called a second time for the special teams to go to the field, he still wasn't ready.

"Why aren't you dressed?" I asked him.

"Man, look at us," he said, frustrated. "We're getting dressed in a *bathroom*." His words were dripping with attitude.

"You don't need to worry about playing today," I yelled. "I have players who *want* to play. We'll be all right without you." He didn't say anything. He just walked off in a huff.

We jumped out to a 17-7 first-quarter lead. Then the mistakes started to happen. Our long-snapper snapped the ball over the punter's head, and they recovered the ball inside our ten-yard line. They scored two plays later. Still, we went to halftime leading 17-15. In the second half, I told our offensive coordinator to keep running the ball because they couldn't stop us. But on the next play, he called a pass and it was intercepted at midfield. I looked at our offensive coordinator, took a deep breath, turned, and walked away. They quickly scored another touchdown to go ahead 22-17. We got the ball back and were driving down the field. I told my offensive coordinator to take out the running back who was in the game because I knew he was prone to fumbling the ball. The offensive coordinator said he wanted to leave him in for one

A Coach's Faith

more play. On the next play, the running back fumbled on our opponent's 15-yard line. I was fuming.

"When I tell you to make a personnel change or call a play," I said sternly, trying to keep my composure, "just do it."

"Do *you* want to call the plays?" he asked sarcastically, making a gesture to hand me his play sheet.

"No, I just want you to listen," I said.

"I've never been so disrespected by a coach in my life," he said angrily. Then he walked to the other end of the bench. We went on to lose the game 41-17 and three of our key players for the season due to injury. After the game, I called a coaches' meeting for Wednesday morning.

At that meeting, I told the staff that I had been thinking and praying about what had happened over the weekend.

"Look, guys," I said calmly, "this is a part-time job for you. But for me, it's my living. As the head coach, if I get fired, all of you are going to get fired, too. But *you* have something to fall back on. I don't. This is it for me. If you don't want to be a part of my system, let me know. If you do, let's go forward and do this thing the right way." Everyone nodded, including my offensive coordinator. Afterwards, he and I met privately, and he agreed to abide by my decisions in the future.

Chapter 20

Our next game would be the school's first homecoming game ever. Our opponent was Southern Tech from Charlotte, North Carolina. In our previous game, we had lost both of our starting offensive tackles, our tight end/long-snapper, our starting weak side linebacker for the season, and I had kicked our best running back off the team. So we had to rework our entire offensive line and play some inexperienced players. At noon on Wednesday, the new coaches' poll came out, and somehow we were still ranked Number 1 with a 5-2 record.

Sunday afternoon was a perfect October day. The homecoming committee had done an excellent job of putting on a pre-game tailgate, and our players went out and mingled with the crowd. It was a great college football atmosphere. The Fellowship of Christian Athletes sent a great speaker to talk to our team before the game. God could not have given us better weather for the game. It was one of our better efforts of the season, and we got a much-needed 26-10 win to push our record to 6-2.

When the Week 7 coaches' poll came out, we had held on to our Number 1 ranking. The following Saturday would be our big matchup with Georgia Military College, a nationally ranked junior college. We knew this would be a tough game, and we would be going into it banged up. On game day, we only dressed out 38 of our 53 players. I told our team that victory for us would not come from the score but how well we competed. I said we had been talking all season about having the faith of a mustard seed to move the mountain. Georgia Military College was our mountain. We lost the game 45-0. But we competed. We were badly undermanned—they dressed 65 players to our 38—and playing a superior team, so in my mind, the mountain was moved.

Week 10 was our last game of the season, and we were scheduled to play the defending National Club Football

A Coach's Faith

Association 2010 National Champs, the University of New Orleans. We had a good week of practice leading up to the game. They were ranked Number 5 at the time, so we knew they didn't have chance of winning the national championship. Their goal was to play spoiler and hurt our chances for the national championship. Even though we lost to Georgia Military College, we were still ranked Number 1. The game felt like we went to a boxing match and a football game broke out. We took an early 21-0 lead in the first quarter, but every chance they got, they were taking cheap shots at our players. Halfway through the third quarter, one of our defensive back and one of their receivers got into it. Both benches cleared. Once the referees got things under control they ejected three of their players and two of ours, and warned both coaches that if it happened again, they would call the game. We ended up winning 51-6 to take our final record to 7-3. We had done all we could do.

Meanwhile, the University of Vermont was ranked Number 3 with a 5-0 record, but still had two games to play.

Tim Freeman

Orangeburg-Calhoun Tech was ranked Number 2, finishing with an 8-2 record. There was one more coaches' poll before the national champs would be crowned. Vermont won their next game but lost the second one to finish the season 6-1. To add to the stress of waiting, I got a call from the league president the week after our final game asking about the fight we had with New Orleans. He asked why I hadn't filed a report about the players being ejected. He told me that the other coach had not done so, either. I apologized for not filing a report, but I also told him that the other team had provoked the fights. I suggested he go on the Internet and watch a replay of the game, and he said he would. He called me the next day and said he had watched the whole game and agreed that they had started the fights. That was the good news. But then he said he was going to place both teams on probation for the remainder of the school year. I immediately asked him if being on probation would prevent us from being named national champion. He said no. That was all I cared about.

A Coach's Faith

Now that our season was over, our coaching staff was already recruiting for the 2012 season. On the day the coaches' poll was to come out, I was on I-285 heading to the Dekalb County recruiting fair when I got a call from an area code I didn't recognize. Thinking it was probably a bill collector, I almost didn't answer. But I did. It was Sandy Sanderson, the league president.

"You got a minute?" he asked.

"Yes," I said, wondering what this was about.

"I just wanted to call and congratulate you on winning the NCFA National Championship!" The first emotion I felt was relief. We had played our last game three weeks ago, and the waiting was killing me. Then I felt pure joy.

"Thank you, sir!" I said. Tears were starting to form in my eyes.

"We're about to post it on the Web site, but I wanted you to be the first to know."

Tim Freeman

I thanked him again and hung up the phone. I started praising God and thanking him for his mercy and grace through the years. There is a group of people I've known who have passed on, and I knew their spirit had been with me through all my trials. I started calling out their names and saying, "We did it!" Then I called my wife. She was so excited. Then I called David Archer, our athletic coordinator. Next I called Coach Hailey to tell him to post it on the team's Facebook page. It was the biggest championship I had ever won. Glory be to God! Amen, Amen, Amen!

Epilogue

Our championship season was in 2011. In January of 2013, I was informed that the school was dropping its football program as part of a reorganization of the athletic department. My first thought was, *Why did God take me out of my own program to spend three years here only to see it come to an abrupt end?* After I had done a lot of praying and meditating, God showed me all the things I had learned during that time. I had learned the inner workings of a college, including how the admissions process worked and the ins and outs of financial aid. It also opened my eyes to see exactly the kind of support system kids needed to be successful in college. These things would serve me well moving forward. God had also shown me that I had touched lives, through such things as huddle meetings with the Fellowship of Christian Athletes and Bible studies with our chaplain. Many of these kids came to Christ as a result, which was my ultimate goal.

Since January of 2013 I have been building a new football program that I feel will be even more successful because God has seen to it that I am now better equipped to do so. At this writing, we have completed our first season. The primary goal of our program is to build young men spiritually, academically, and athletically so they will make better husbands, fathers, and community leaders. It is my personal goal to bring as many of them to Christ as I can. I am so thankful that God often uses the most unlikely people to accomplish his purposes. God has given each of us a special gift for his purpose of being Christ-like and furthering his kingdom on earth.

How do you find out what your purpose is? Everyone is passionate about something. My passion is football, and I use it as an opportunity to tell young men about Jesus. Likewise, you can use whatever you are passionate about to tell people about God's goodness. Everyone has testimony--a story about how God brought them through a tough time. Use yours to encourage others. You don't have to be a church leader to lead to people to God. All you have to do is be an example of God's love and grace each day of your life. You

A Coach's Faith

will be surprised at how many lives you touch without even trying. People are watching you even when you don't know they're watching. Matthew 6:33 says, "But seek ye first the kingdom of God, and his righteousness; and all these things shall be added unto you." All you have to do is seek God. Read your Bible to seek God's wisdom. Listen for God. He will often speak to you at the oddest times.

    I once heard a pastor say that when you wake up at 3 a.m. and can't sleep, get a pencil and paper and listen for God to speak to your spirit. Then write down what your spirit tells you. Always listen for God in conversations with people. God will tell you directly what he wants you to do. He may confirm his will for you through the words of someone else. I'm not talking about people who walk up to you and say out of the blue, "God told me to tell you to move across country." I'm talking about when God speaks to your spirit about what he wants you to do rather than someone who really has no idea of what God wants you to do.

Tim Freeman

When I work with kids, I always tell them to walk by faith and not by sight. But to do this, you need to understand what faith is. About eight years ago, I put the following series of verses together when I was going through a difficult time in my life. I searched the Bible for verses that talked about faith and put together what I call the Seven Days of Faith. Each week, I would study these verses one day at a time. Then I applied that verse to a specific challenge I was facing. Over the years, this has helped me grow in faith.

Seven Days of Faith

In going through times of adversity, I developed the following process to help build me up to be able to do what God has called me to do. My hope is that these verses help you accomplish God's purposes in your life:

Day 1--The meaning of FAITH.

Hebrews 11:1: "Now Faith is the substance of things hoped for and the evidence of thing not yet seen."

Day 2--How we should walk DAILY.

2 Corinthians 5:7: "For we walk by FAITH, not by sight."

Day 3--You have to put some WORK in what you do.

James 2:14: "Faith without works is DEAD. What does it profit, my brethren, if someone says he has faith but does not have works? Can faith save him?"

Day 4--Dare yourself to do the IMPOSSIBLE.

Matthew 17:20: "So Jesus said to them, 'Because of your unbelief; for assuredly I say to you, if you have faith the size of a Mustard seed, you will say to this Mountain, Move from here to there, and it will move, and **NOTHING** will be impossible for you.'"

Day 5--Study the word of God DAILY.

Romans 10:17: "So then faith comes by hearing, and hearing by the word of God."

Day 6--BELIEVE God will reward you.

Hebrews 11:6: "But without faith it is impossible to please him, for he who comes to God must believe that he is, and that he is a REWARDER of those who diligently seek him."

Day 7--DO NOT give up on your VISION, DREAMS, or PURPOSE

2 Timothy 4:7: "I have fought the good fight, I have finished the race, I have kept the FAITH."

About the Author

Tim Freeman spent three seasons (2010-2012) as head coach of the Chattahoochee Tech College football program, which won the 2011National Club Football Association Championship. Prior to that, Freeman was athletic director of the Cobb Saints Sports Academy in Marietta, Georgia, an independent football program for student athletes who did not qualify academically to play football as a college freshman. In 2008, he served as head coach for the Northside Christian Athletics Lions, a high school program for home-schooled student athletes. He spent 2007 as athletic coordinator and offensive line coach for the Ware Prep Academy post-graduate football program in Atlanta. Freeman was also the founder and athletic director of Mt. Olive Prep Academy (2001-04) and North Atlanta Prep Academy (2004-06), where he built two nationally recognized high school post-graduate basketball programs. Freeman is a native of Duluth, Ga., and attended Livingston University in Alabama. He currently is

Tim Freeman

founder and director of the North Georgia Sports Academy in Cornelia, Ga.

Praise for Coach Freeman

The two years I spent at Chattahoochee Tech helped me in a number of ways. The school and staff helped me get my grades back to where they were supposed to be and reminded me of the importance grades play on all my decisions. I believe junior college is a great way for people to get ready for college and the experiences that they are going to go through. Sports also helped me transition to a four-year school. Football helped me realize that there are great players at all levels of sports and that the same goes for a coaching staff. If you listen to the coaches, then you will do well, but if you don't, more than likely things will turn out worse than expected. The same goes for track at the junior college level. It's a great way to test your skill against the different levels in college to see where you would fit in best. After two years at Chattahoochee Tech, I was able to walk away with a scholarship to Western Kentucky, an associated degree in business management, and the knowledge of what to expect at the next stage in my life. I would recommend junior college

Tim Freeman

to anyone who is not quite ready for a four-year school or hasn't decided what they want to do with their lives.

--Cedric Stadom

Chattahoochee Technical College 2011-2013,

Western Kentucky University

Junior college gave me a second chance to re-establish my academic GPA and another opportunity to play football at the next level. Junior college is very important because it allows you to get to where you want to be in furthering your education and sport of choice. It also gives a student an opportunity to meet their financial needs through grants and scholarships. While at junior college I played football which helped me to refocus my desire to work hard and play football at the next level. Programs like this are needed to give students a second chance to make a difference. There is more one on one attention with teachers and coaches to get you ready for the next step in your life; whether it's a four year college or the work force. Without junior colleges there

A Coach's Faith

would be a much higher ratio of dropouts at the college level and wouldn't give students a chance at higher education.

--Morgan Wright

Chattahoochee Technical College 2011-2013,

Tusculum College

I attended North Atlanta Prep Academy in 2005-06; I must say it was the best decision I have ever made. Not graduating from high school due to the graduation test really hurt my chances of going to college, but without Tim Freeman and North Atlanta Prep I wouldn't have graduated with my diploma nor have received a full-scholarship to attend Howard College, which was ranked as the #1 junior college in the country when I signed to play there the following year. Mr. Tim Freeman and North Atlanta Prep made me believe that nothing is impossible! Therefore, since then I have graduated with an associate's degree and most recent with a Business degree. I also finished my playing career at Point University and then played professionally in the China,

Tim Freeman

Uruguay, and Brazil. I am 27 years old, and now I am the player representative for the MSA International Sports Agency based in Tampa, Florida. Attending North Atlanta Prep was a blessing!

--Shasta Scott

North Atlanta Prep Academy 2005-06,

Howard College Junior College, Point University

Words cannot express my gratitude for Coach Tim Freeman and what his program did for me. For a guy like me, it was a second chance, maybe even a last chance. The program pushed me academically, and I was able to make qualifying scores on my SATs. The program's visibility throughout the southeast helped me get a full scholarship to Fayetteville State University in North Carolina. Coach Freeman's vision and willingness to help kids achieve is beyond measure. I would recommend his program to any student athlete who needs an opportunity.

--James Draine

A Coach's Faith

Mt. Olive Prep Academy 2003-2004,

Fayetteville State University

Having a football program at the junior college level helps athletes coming out of high school who suffer because their classroom efforts were below standards or field performance wasn't just what they were looking for. Also, some individuals fall victim to negative peer pressure from friends, family, and the community. But as we get older, we can learn from our mistakes and try to make things right. Fortunately, the junior college program gives hope to those wanting to make a comeback and want to make their next steps memorable.

--Teron Williams

Chattahoochee Tech 211-2013,

Clark Atlanta University

Where are they now 2002-2012?

2002

Tim Brown, United States Army, Basketball

Brian Giddens. Devry Institute of Technology, Basketball

Carl Muldrow, West Georgia College, Basketball

Tim Hutchins, Southwest Oregon Community College, Montana State-Northern, Basketball

Jabar Langford, City College of Pennsylvania, Basketball

Shanchez Thomas, Devry Institute of Technology, Basketball

Josh Hood, St. Johns Community College, Basketball

Merva Johnson, West Georgia College, Basketball

Terry Hunter, Gordon College, Basketball

2003

Shan Finley, Panola Junior College, Texas A&M, Basketball

Lance Tippet, Chattanooga State Community College, Miles College, Basketball

Tim Freeman

Brooks Smith, Gadsden State Community College, Albany State, Basketball

Moussa Diagne, Furman University, Basketball

Chris Ellis, Georgia Southwestern, Basketball

Tyrece Lettgett, Alabama State University, Basketball

Richard Lott, Alabama State University, Basketball

Leland Mapp, California Junior College, Basketball

James Pasley, United States Air Force, Basketball

Kevin Millis, Chattahoochee Tech, Basketball

2004

Chron Tatum, Riverside Community College, Idaho, Basketball

Angel Alamo, Riverside Community College, Sacramento State, Basketball

Ra'Shun Bryan, Tennessee Tech, Basketball

Adrian Beasley, Free Will Baptist Bible College, Basketball

J.R. Williams, Ohio Junior College, Basketball

James Draine, Atlanta Metro Tech, Basketball

A Coach's Faith

Juan Ornelas, Virginia Intermont College, Basketball

Josh Coppin, Lane College, Basketball

Kenny Keenan, Clark Atlanta Univ., Basketball

2005

Chad Jones, Morehouse College, Basketball

Dominique Bedford, Kennesaw State University, Basketball

Antoine Taylor, Kennesaw State University, Basketball

Courtnei Houston, Georgia Southern University, Basketball

Paul Daniels, Bluefield College, Reinhardt College, Basketball

Rashad Brown, Southwest Texas Christian College, Texas A&M-Commerce, Basketball

2006

Jonathan Belt, Alabama A&M, Clark Atlanta University, Basketball

Kevin Lott, Georgia State University, Basketball

Chad Wynn, East Carolina University, Basketball

Tim Freeman

Kensha Johnson, Coastal Georgia, South Carolina State, Basketball

Shasta College, Howard College, Atlanta Metro College, Basketball

Zach Daniels, New Mexico Military College, Basketball

2007

Jimmy Oden, Lipscomb University, Middle Tennessee State, Basketball

Stephen Kite, Mississippi Valley State University, Basketball

Hillary Haley, St. Bonaventure University, University of Maryland Eastern Shore, Basketball

Josh Smith, Presbyterian College, Basketball

Brittion Smith, East Mississippi Community College, Mars Hill, Basketball

Jeff Smith, Wallace State Community College, Mercer, Basketball

Chris Hines, Illinois Community College, Alabama, Basketball

A Coach's Faith

Javaris Blue, Louisburg College, Football

Wesley Journey, Louisburg College, Football

Derek Finch, Louisburg College, West Georgia, Football

Michael Mcray, Dean College, Football

Andre Hayward, Dean College, Football

Jeff Terrell, Grand Rapids Community College, Football

Ron Ward, Eastern Arizona, Concordia (AL), Football

Johnny Lee Dixon, Pearl River Community College, Canadian Football League, Football

Gerald Boston, Edward Waters College, Football

Adam Davis, Coffeeville Community College, Kansas State, Football

Demarlo Belcher, Indiana University, Football

Bruce Irvin, Mt. San Antonio College, West Virginia, Football

Tim Freeman

2009

Juan Hector, Concordia (Alabama), Football

Danny White, Carson-Newman, Football

Derrick Allen Jr., Avila University, Football

Julian Gardner III, Georgia State (walk on), Football

James Ferguson, Louisburg College, Football

Marcus Cabiness, Albany State, Football

Anthony Leonard, Alabama State, Football

Rakeem Bell, Louisburg College, Football

Torrance McMillin, Louisburg College, Football

Ian Rump, Louisburg College, Football

2010

Tyler Deihl, Presbyterian College, Basketball

Brandon Farmer, Allen University, Basketball

Larry Harden, Morehouse College, Basketball

Chris Randolph, Johnson C. Smith, Football

Jake Schmidt, Shorter College, Football

A Coach's Faith

2011

Jamal Hunte, Point University, Pikeville College, Football

Marvon Danzie, Fort Valley State, Football

Kenneth Preston, Fort Valley State, Football

2012

Morgan Alexander, Pikeville University, Football

Morgan Wright, Tusculum College, Football

Cedric Stadom, Western Kentucky, Football & Track

Steven Johnson, University of the Cumberland, Football & Track

D're Gibson, University of the Cumberlands, Football & Track

Albert Catron, Georgia Rampage, Arena Football

Alfred Hughly, Atlanta Sharks, Arena Football

To order more books
Or to contact Coach Freeman,
visit: www.TimFreemanSr.com

www.ingramcontent.com/pod-product-compliance
Lightning Source LLC
LaVergne TN
LVHW021714060526
838200LV00050B/2657